SQUEEZE
THE JUICE
OUT OF LIFE!

MW00457101

GETTING
PAID
to play with
PUPPIES

Creating a Career and Life You Love

By

FERNANDO CAMACHO

Interior book design by Fernando Camacho and Vasudeva Rao H.

Cover photographs and design by Peter Gargiulo

Editing by Rebecca Shipman

Proofreading by Christine Gossinger

Table of Contents

Join The Revolution

The book you're about to read contains ideas. And these ideas will cause you to think about yourself and your life. That thinking might lead you to a desire to make some changes in your life - changes you know deep down are for the better.

The problem with change is that it's unknown and can be quite difficult. We're all creatures of habit and tend to do what we've always done before - defaulting to our norm - even if it's not good for us. This makes the thought of change easy; however, the action of change is a challenge.

Small changes though, aren't too much of a stretch for us to make. By just tweaking a few things in our lives we can effectively switch from one thing to another, like changing your hair gel or what you order at Starbucks. That's easy.

Big life changes, like we'll be discussing in this book, will not be as easy. They may cause you to take big leaps of faith, adopt totally different mindsets and put yourself in uncomfortable situations. No, big change is not easy.

However, big life changes can lead to amazingly huge rewards. They have the ability to totally transform you as a person and direct you to great levels of happiness and fulfillment. That's why it's so important for you to open your mind to new possibilities and have the strength to make it happen for you.

Big change is something that's painfully hard without support. To try to change some major facet of your life; to do something totally new and different, is damn hard. Not impossible, but generally a pain in the butt, uphill battle that will cause most people to give up before they ever see it through.

My advice: don't go it alone.

You need people around you who will talk you through the scary parts, offer encouragement as you take bold new steps forward and who will be there when you fall flat on your face (which may happen from time to time - or all the time if you're me.) Having a supportive group of people who understand what you're going through, who will never judge you and are eager to lend a helping hand just when you need it most, will make your journey so much more pleasurable and stack the deck in your favor.

Since finding such an understanding and super cool group of people is tough, I would like to personally invite you to a special group of game-changers that is ready and waiting to help you do whatever you need to do to improve your life. You're not alone, so you shouldn't do this alone. There are so many people just like you who crave more out of their life and just need a little support to make it happen.

Your admission to this elite group is absolutely free of charge, but does come with one condition. You have to pledge to be honest, allow yourself to be vulnerable and to always help others along the way. If you can do that, you will love our tribe and soon become a valuable part of our community.

We call ourselves The Happiness Freedom Fighters (HFF).

You see, happiness is too important to go after passively. I see too many people who want a better job or would like to improve their life in some way, but they aren't going after it with any real effort or passion. Happiness is not something that will just accidentally fall out of the sky and land in your lap - you have to aggressively fight for it.

I'm talking about a revolution against mediocrity; an uprising against settling for less than you deserve and a spark to ignite the fire in your soul.

Okay, I feel like I'm making it sound a lot like a cult. But it's really just a great group of people who are more than happy to support you as you take the steps to improve your life. The focus of this book is to help you create a rewarding career that will bring you happiness every day you do it, but the HFF is about working on upping the joy-o-meter in all areas of your life.

We share our experiences and are there for one another to answer questions, provide guidance and/or give you a big kick in the backside when you need it. In addition to the amazing support you'll receive from the community, I'll be there with whatever help I can give you. I also provide some bonus video content that will both expand and reinforce the principals we're about to discuss in this book.

Once again, it's 100% free and will only help you take the actions needed to put more smiles in your future. Just go to www.happinessfreedomfighters.com and join the happiness revolution.

Hope to see you there.

Freedom Fighters Unite!

Fern

Introduction

What brought you here?

I mean here in your career, in your life and here reading this book.

Is it because you're not quite satisfied with your current job?

Is it because you wish you felt more fulfilled in life?

Or maybe it's just because I sucked you in by putting a cute puppy on the cover.

No matter the reason, I'm glad you're here. My hope is that this book will in some way (or many ways) improve the quality of your life. That's a simple, yet bold expectation for me and one I've thought about for quite some time.

You see, at some point I've been where you are. Now, I don't pretend to know your exact circumstances or understand the specifics of your current situation, but I'm pretty sure I've felt like you do right now at some point.

We tend to think that we're all so different and that no one can truly know what we're going through or how we really feel, but in the end we're all the same. We all go through our own stuff - both good and bad - and have to figure out a way to make sense of it all and get the most out of our time here. Although the details will vary from person to person, the themes are exactly the same.

I've been utterly depressed and insanely happy. I've broken down to tears before and also laughed so hard that water came out my nose. I've felt isolated and alone, but also comforted by a loving community. I've been happy and I've been sad, had hard times and also amazing encounters. Just like you.

I'm not a guru and I don't pretend to have all the answers - that's not what this book is about. I'm just a guy who's now reflecting on the events of my life, inspecting my experiences and sharing the big lessons that I've learned now that I'm almost halfway through (I'm currently 48 and, yes, I plan on hitting 100). Our lives are so precious but terribly fleeting, so we need to get the most out of every minute and be intentional about how we steer them.

I made a decision years ago to never spend any prolonged time doing things that did not make me happy and it's served me well. I'm happier today than I've ever been in my life. I look forward to getting up each morning and can't wait to see what's next for me because life just keeps getting better every day, every year. I didn't always feel this way. In fact, I actually used to feel the polar opposite - depressed, unhappy and dreading the rise of each day. Not fun.

Of all the things I discuss in this book, there's one point that I want you to take in above all others: DON'T SETTLE. Don't accept a life less than what you want. Don't stop trying to achieve your dreams. Don't let another year go by feeling unfulfilled. Don't sit back and watch others doing the things you want to do. Don't you dare settle for less than you want and deserve.

I don't know you. I don't know where you are or what you've gone through, but in a little while you'll know me. You'll know where I am now as well as what I've been through. I'm going to do my best to share what I've learned in transforming my career, my state of mind and my life in hopes that you can use my experiences and the lessons I've learned to up the happiness in your own life.

I can't promise that after reading this book you'll land the job of your dreams and ride off into the sunset on a rainbow colored unicorn, BUT I will give you something to think about and maybe, just maybe, you'll take action on a few things that will bring more smiles to your days.

Okay, now let me tell you a story . . .

1

This Is Why I Do It

I was kind of surprised to see her crying. This was our second session together and we had been working with her dog for only about ten minutes this afternoon. To me, nothing really special had happened – her dog, a tall Black Mouth Cur named Sandy, had just walked up a short stairway leading to a small office building. It was something so simple, however to my client it was a major accomplishment.

Elizabeth had adopted Sandy about five months earlier and had already formed a great bond with her and couldn't imagine life without her. Sandy is a super sweet and affectionate dog who loves everyone she meets. Immediately after adopting her, however, Elizabeth noticed that Sandy had a few issues.

When you adopt a dog from a rescue or shelter you don't always know where they came from or what they've been through in their life before meeting you. Their current behavior has been shaped by past experiences, both good and bad. Many people incorrectly assume that rescue dogs are damaged or flawed but that's usually not the case at all. Most of the time, they are just good dogs that have had some bad luck or haven't yet found the right match.

We'll never know what happened to Sandy or any rescue dog with no recorded history. I always say your dog's life begins the day you adopt them. Although they come to you with some habits (both good and bad), dogs live in the present moment and are very capable of changing and developing new habits (also both good and bad).

If I had to guess, I would say that Sandy lived in a loving home at some point but was either not socialized properly when she was a puppy and/or spent most of her time in a ranch style home without stairways. Because she probably never had early experiences going up or down stairs, she doesn't know she can do it and has become fearful of using them. She is also nervous and very reluctant to go through certain doorways, especially unfamiliar ones.

Elizabeth lives in a beautiful three story, Victorian house that has plenty of space for a large dog to wander around and enjoy. Of all the places in her home, Elizabeth spends the most time on the third floor, where she has an office and lovely sitting room. She wanted a dog to keep her company and spend their days together on the top level while Elizabeth got some stuff done.

When she first brought Sandy home, she wouldn't go up any of the stairs. However, after encouraging her over the first couple of months, Sandy learned to climb the first floor of stairs with no problem, but was still petrified of going up the narrow and slightly steeper stairway going up to the third floor. In addition, Sandy wouldn't go through the alleyway that leads from the parking lot to the vet's office. Elizabeth would have to call and have a vet technician come out and carry Sandy into the office, which was stressful for Sandy and, at about 65 pounds, not a lot of fun for the vet techs either.

That's why I ended up getting the call for help. I was hired to help Sandy get over her fears, build her confidence and enable she & Elizabeth to live together better. I was more than happy to take the job – this is my favorite kind of client. I love to work on anxieties with dogs. It breaks my heart to see a dog suffering and not enjoying life to the fullest. Each day that a dog spends in any state of anxiety diminishes their quality of life, which in turn, affects the pet parent's quality of life. So when I heard about Sandy's issues, I was eager to get started and see how I could help this awesome dog.

Treating anxiety can sometimes be a long and slow process. You have to proceed slowly and only at the dog's pace, making sure not to push too hard, too soon. If you rush it, you risk doing more harm than good which can actually make the anxiety worse – not good.

My first session with Sandy was at their home where we discussed their brief life together and I learned as much as I could about what Sandy is like, the progress they've made and what struggles they were having. I like to start all my private behavioral sessions in the home, if possible - this is where they spend the most time, where the dog is the most comfortable and where I can get a good feel for their relationship and what's really going on.

Being a behavior specialist is a lot like being a detective. You have to get as much information as possible, piece together the clues and figure out what's really going on (which may be very different than what the client tells you), and then put together a treatment plan that is customized for the individual person, dog, situation and lifestyle. This is one of my favorite parts about my job and one of the main reasons I decided to stop teaching group obedience classes and just focus on in-home consultations. I love the investigative process and figuring out the best way to reach a dog and the best tools to give the humans involved to improve their situation.

It's so rewarding to be able to come to the aid of someone who's struggling and help them improve their life. I think being of service to others is just the best way to earn a living – and as a bonus, I get to help dogs as well – pretty damn cool.

During that first session with Sandy, I took her for a walk and interacted with her in her home a bit to get a sense of her personality and see what her general behavior was like. I immediately found her to be an extremely fun and loving dog, quick to give a wag of her tail and generous with the licks to the face - my kind of dog for sure.

After observing and working with her for about an hour, I could see absolutely no signs of anxiety at all. She moved with ease and didn't seem fearful with anything. Then, Elizabeth and I went up to the third floor. It was obvious that Sandy wanted to stay with us as we climbed the stairs, but it was as if there was an invisible wall stopping her from moving forward and up the first step. She shuffled back and forth in uncertainty and kept looking up at us, darting her eyes back and forth along the first few stairs in front of her.

I knew she was physically capable of walking up the stairs – she flies up the first floor stairs to get to the second level but has some sort of irrational fear of even attempting the next flight. I tried everything I could think of to get Sandy to give those stairs a try but with no luck. I used freeze dried liver to lure her up and was able to get her to lean forward to reach out for the food, but she wouldn't step up. I then tried to appeal to her goofy, playful side and got her favorite toy. I used my patented, high-pitched puppy voice and ran her up the first floor and at full-speed to the second set of stairs, hoping our momentum would get her past that invisible wall she had put up. Nothing worked.

Disappointed but not deterred, I suggested we try working on some of the other locations she has trouble with. This time I was going to bring out the big guns, something I had a feeling would be much more motivating than food, toys or my irresistible puppy voice – another dog.

After my failure at the home, my client was a bit dejected, feeling like Sandy would never get over her fear of stairs. She was sad because, although she would never give Sandy up, she couldn't enjoy the life she wanted to with her. There was so much Sandy and she couldn't do because of Sandy's fears and it made a lot of things, like going to the vet, very difficult.

She also needed someplace for Sandy to stay when she occasionally traveled. Ideally, she wanted Sandy to stay with her niece who loves her, but her niece lives in a third floor, walkup apartment where Sandy refused to even set foot through the main doorway to the building.

For this second session, we met on a residential side street a few blocks from the vet's office. I had my buddy Spencer bring his dog, Ziggy to go for a walk with us and see if Sandy would soak up some of Ziggy's confidence and try some new things. Ziggy is a shaggy, well-balanced Golden Retriever that we've used a few times before to work with some grumpy dogs. He's playful but calm and, thanks to Spencer, takes direction well.

As soon as Sandy saw Ziggy, her face brightened and her whole body got wiggly. After a happy butt sniffing (the dogs, not us) we started off on a nice, structured walk. We had only gotten about a hundred yards when we hit our first set of stairs that led to a local business. They weren't much, only three wide steps with a handicap ramp on the side, leading to the main doors.

I had Spencer and Ziggy lead the way and walk up the stairs with Sandy and me right behind, followed by Elizabeth. Ziggy happily jogged up the stairs, not understanding he was about to be responsible for something so special. When it was Sandy's turn to go up those few stairs with me, she hesitated as her prior conditioning and habit of being fearful of stairways kicked in, but only for a moment. The next second she was bounding up the stairs, eyes focused on Ziggy and where he was headed next.

As Sandy's feet hit the second stair, I heard Elizabeth gasp in surprise from behind me, followed by a joyous cheer. We paused at the doorway to the building and that's when I noticed my client's eyes were welled up with tears. The depression of what seemed like an impossible task just minutes before was now replaced by a wave of hope and possibilities.

I didn't let the celebration go on for long though. I knew we still had work to do. I had Ziggy move down the handicap ramp and go back up the stairs again. This time around Sandy didn't flinch, she went straight up the stairs after Ziggy. We did that loop a few more times and then I felt it was time for the next challenge.

We continued walking and found another set of stairs leading up to a back door of another business. This set of stairs was very different. These weren't cement, they were wood. It wasn't only three steps, it was about thirty. They weren't wide, they were narrow. The first set of stairs was Sandy's training wheels, now it was time to let go and see what she would do.

Up she went, following Ziggy with no reservations whatsoever. She took them like she had been doing them for years without the slightest hint that she was uncomfortable. Again, my client cheered with delight. But I wasn't done yet.

We headed to the alleyway that led from the parking lot to the vet's office. Never had Sandy gone down that dark walkway on her own four paws; she always had to be carried in. I was now very confident that we could get Sandy to do any set of stairs, but this was a different stimulus and a separate trigger of anxiety, so all bets were off.

As we approached the alley, I watched Sandy in the corner of my eye to see how she would respond. Just like with the stairs, I had Spencer and Ziggy lead, with Sandy and myself right on their heels and tail. Although I've worked with similar issues before and was encouraged by our earlier success, I really didn't know what Sandy was going to do as we moved forward.

Although it was dark and you could hear the noises of the busy street on the other end of the alley echoing off the walls, Sandy went right in without slowing a bit. She looked happy as she looked from Ziggy to the surrounding environment. No fear at all. This caused an "Oh my God, I don't believe it," from Elizabeth as we moved straight though the alleyway, made a quick turn down the sidewalk and went right into the vet's office.

Inside we said "hi" to the receptionist and the one person sitting in the waiting room, explained what we were doing and then walked out. Once we got back outside, I looked over to Elizabeth who had become strangely silent. She was speechless, staring down at Sandy as if she didn't recognize this strange dog. We were on a roll, but I still wasn't done.

Next we headed to her niece's apartment building. The three-story building was narrow and old, but in good shape. The front door opened into a very small, cramped foyer that barely allowed you to step inside before you hit the second door that allowed access to the apartments. Looking in, I could see that the inside hallway was dark and led immediately to a staircase going up. Seeing how tight of a space the foyer was made me think this might be a bit challenging for Sandy, who doesn't like cramped doorways, let alone the stairs beyond.

I was feeling good after our recent successes though, so we went right for it, using the same system: Spencer and Ziggy leading the way, with Sandy and I close behind. Ziggy went right in, but as soon as we got to the first doorway, Sandy froze and wouldn't budge. I had Spencer and Ziggy come back out and got them fired up and encouraged them to play a little bit right there in front of the building while we still held on to their leashes.

After about a minute of them happily engaging each other while we did "the leash dance" (that familiar routine people with playful dogs meeting on leash become experts at), we headed toward the main door again. As before, Spencer and Ziggy went in first and once again, Sandy hesitated when it was our turn, but I kept going and gave the leash a short, but firm pull and release – not a hard yank – just a firm nudge to get her wheels moving.

It worked! Sandy went through not only the first door, but through the second and up the first flight of stairs to join Ziggy, who was waiting there for her. We cheered a bit there then went back outside to do it again. This time, Sandy went through the doorway with very minimal hesitation. I made her do just the doorways and the first flight of stairs a few more times, making sure we got to the point where she showed no signs of anxiety. Then, we took on the next two flights, which she did pretty easily.

Every time you succeed in overcoming a trigger of fear, you create a more confident dog overall, making new challenges a little easier to deal with. That's why when I work with anxious dogs, I always first look for some issues that we can improve easily and get some quick wins to build momentum. Our earlier work and repetitions had made Sandy open to the possibility that there was nothing to fear in these situations she once thought so frightening.

We spent some time in her niece's apartment, doing a happy dance and letting Sandy check out the place where she would now spend time whenever Elizabeth had to travel. I can't explain how amazing it felt to see Elizabeth smile widely with such relief and joy on her face. She was so appreciative and couldn't thank us enough.

The relative ease at which Sandy overcame fear after fear in such a short period of time made me appear like a dog training God.

I spent about a second basking in my greatness, then admitted the truth and explained how it was really Ziggy who did it all – I just happened to be there as well. I gave them homework to come back as soon as possible and do all the things we did with Ziggy, so as to build off the fresh, positive experiences, which they did with continued success.

Even with all those recent wins, Sandy still refused to go up to the third floor of her own home and also wouldn't jump into the car, instead waiting to be lifted into it by my client (who should not be lifting a dog that size). So about a month later, I returned with Spencer and Ziggy to finally get Sandy to the top floor.

We followed the same formula, but Sandy was much more reluctant in this situation. We had five months of repetitions of not going up the stairs working against us. Since we were starting inside the house, I initially didn't leash her, thinking the freedom would create less tension. After a few failed attempts, I decided to see if having us go up together as a structured team would help.

As we approached the stairs after Spencer and Ziggy, Sandy balked as usual and I tried the same technique that worked in Elizabeth niece's doorway – a quick, but firm tug on the leash as I kept moving confidently up the stairs. I had to use a little more effort because we were going up, but it worked just the same.

As soon as Sandy took the first (most difficult for her) step forward, she realized she could do it and there was nothing really to be afraid of. She never needed any more assistance or convincing to do those stairs again. Now, she gallops up and down with enthusiasm with those old anxieties long forgotten and she spends all day lounging with Elizabeth on the third floor.

Spencer, Ziggy and I didn't stop there that day. We then went out to the driveway and quickly got Sandy in and out of the car on her own. I'm not sure what made me happier, the look on Elizabeth's face when Sandy first did the stairs or the glee in which Sandy now runs up and down them.

This is why I jump up every morning, excited to get to work. I love my job and feel so blessed to be able to do something I enjoy so much, every single day. I see people all around me, head down on their way to work like they're walking into detention or being sent to their room without supper. They look (and feel) like their getting punished.

That sucks.

Considering we only get one shot at life, don't you think you should spend your time doing things you enjoy?

Hell yeah! And you can. You can have a job you love and spend your working hours on this planet doing great work that makes you smile every single day. I've heard people say that it's not possible, that it's "called work because you're not supposed to like it." I disagree, big time. You can and you should do work you love.

The other thing people will say is, "you can't make money doing what you love." Wrong again! In every profession you can think of, there are people doing it really well and making good money doing it. There's also a whole bunch of people who are doing it poorly and are struggling. You just have to decide which group you want to fall into and then make it happen.

Sound easy? Well, it's not. If it was easy, everyone would have their dream job. Those who are unable to make it happen either don't know the steps to take, lack the motivation and/or give up WAY too easily. The path and the tools are available to everyone if you get the right information and take action. That's what I'm going to help you with in this book.

No, it's not easy - at least it wasn't for me, but I'm here to tell you it is WELL worth the effort.

2

Finding Your Path

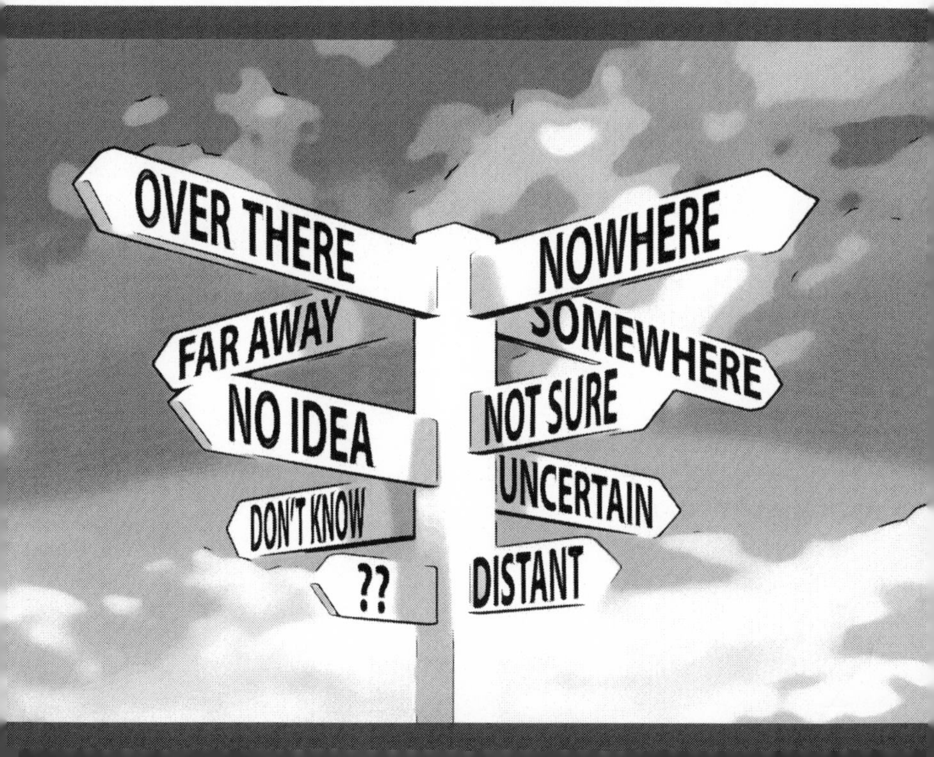
OVER THERE
NOWHERE
FAR AWAY
SOMEWHERE
NO IDEA
NOT SURE
DON'T KNOW
UNCERTAIN
??
DISTANT

The guy didn't mean to be an insensitive jerk with his seemingly polite comment, but that's kind of what I thought of him as he said it to me.

The year was 2002 and I was at a backyard party at a family friend's house enjoying a nice summer afternoon of free food and nice conversation. I had just finished taking down a big plate of grilled chicken and potato salad, feeling pretty good about my full belly and the warm sunshine cascading down on me, when I was approached by this guy and his wife. The couple was all smiles as they walked up to me and made the comment that I knew was coming and silently dreaded.

Over the years, more than a few different people have said it to me at all kinds of family events. Even though it happened so often and I expected it, it still kind of pisses me off every single time. I know it's never said with the intent to make me feel badly (although it always did) or that the people saying it had any idea how it affected me. They actually meant well. So, although I wasn't thrilled hearing it yet again, I tried not to hold it against them.

"Hi, you must be Fernando's son," (my Dad and I share the same name – I'm a junior) the man said, "... the doctor."

It was actually a pretty honest mistake. My brother Rick and I are only three years apart and do look very much alike (when Rick's son was little he used to think I was Rick all the time and would constantly look for me to pick him up). The problem wasn't that he confused Rick and me, it's what I was forced to say next that kind of stung.

"No, I'm the other son," I replied stoically.

Yup, that's me, "the other son". No, not the doctor. Not the one who's got his life in order. Not the one who's on his way to success. Not the one with initials after his name. No, not me. I'm the other one. I'm the one no one seems to understand. I'm the one that has no idea what he wants to do if he grows up. I'm the one that no one can easily explain. That's me, not the one, the "other one".

That's what went through my head every single time someone said that to me. The reason I felt like this was not because my parents favored my brother Rick over me or that I heard people talking negatively about me. It was my own doing, mostly due to societal perceptions of what success looked like "in the real world" and the subtle pressure it can put on people (namely me). A big factor was also my own insecurities and the never ending conversation going on in my head about my path in life.

Unlike my brother Rick, who knew pretty early on what career path he wanted to take, I had no idea what I wanted to do or what direction I should take. After high school I went to Seton Hall University, just a short twenty-minute ride from my house in Clifton, New Jersey. Since I had no clue as to what I wanted to do, I started college as an undecided major, hoping to figure it out somewhere in my first year there.

Back then (I graduated in 1992), everybody and everything pushed you toward some kind of big business career; something like accounting, sales or marketing. I felt tremendous external pressure to get a suit and tie, drink coffee and buy a brief case. The only problem was that I was pretty sure I hated all of those things. I was more of a t-shirt, fruit juice and backpack kind of guy. I considered myself a creative free spirit that was very much anti-conformity.

This is where one of my biggest frustrations started and one that would continually plague me for years to come. It seemed that every time I was interested in something, somebody came along and explained that it wasn't possible or realistic. They would then point out that the mainstream business world was the place to be and that I needed to follow the herd.

I felt like life was a big game board where we all began at the same start space and then had to move our game pieces down the painted path that the manufacturer had decided was the way you had to go to get to the finish. My problem was that I didn't like the predetermined path I was thrust onto. I liked what I saw off to the left and right of the path. There was a lot of interesting looking stuff over there that I was sure must be more than just decoration. So I would jump the wall and head off the path, but every time I did, someone (my parents, friends, teachers, the media) would pick up my game piece, tell me I couldn't do that – it was against the rules – and place me back on the path.

I would listen for a few more moves, but then something off the path would catch my eye and I would try to head in that direction, only to have my piece picked up and put back on the proper path.

I knew I didn't like where this game was going, but seemed to have no choice but to follow along.

After about a year and a half, if you haven't already done so, the college forces you to pick a major. My problem at the time was I still didn't really know what I wanted to focus on, so I did the only logical thing for me: I picked my major based on what required the least amount of math courses. Math was never my thing. I really didn't understand its value and had a really tough time getting any grade higher than a "C" in any course that had anything to do with numbers. So after looking over my options and their individual requirements, I become a communications major for the start of my junior year.

Although I had finally picked my major, I was still no closer to knowing what that would do for me or what kind of job that would get me post-graduation. I was still a bit lost and unsure of how I was going to use this expensive education my parents were paying for, but knew I had to figure something out soon. People were starting to ask questions – my parents, friends, and it seemed the world needed me to pick a direction and make my future career choice.

There were many resources available to me and no shortage of people with ideas of what I should get into. Ultimately, I turned to one of my most trusted sources for information and guidance at the time - television sitcoms. One of my favorite shows growing up was *Bosom Buddies*, starring Peter Scolari and the then unknown, Tom Hanks. In the show, the two actors needed a place to live and found a great apartment, but the only problem being it was in a building for women only. Of course they did the only logical thing, and dressed like chicks to get the apartment. Hilarity ensued. I loved that show. Still do. If you can find those old episodes somewhere, do yourself a favor and binge watch them one rainy Sunday. You'll thank me.

In the show, Tom and Peter's characters worked in the creative department of an advertising agency. Peter was the copywriter and Tom was the graphic artist. Although Peter played a great part, Tom was my man and I wanted to be just like his character, Kip (minus the cross dressing). That's how I decided to add the minor of advertising art alongside my Communications major. I figured I would become a graphic designer, work in an advertising agency and create catchy ad campaigns that would sell lots of products to people, who all of a sudden felt they needed to have them.

Was this really what I wanted to do?

I had no idea. Maybe. Who knows. I just had to make a choice and felt it was a decent compromise between my creative side and the nudges to do something in business. I don't think my situation was all that unique. I would bet that most people really have no idea what they want to do with their life at age twenty and are struggling with the same questions and reservations in trying to pick a direction to go.

What I now know is that it's not only okay not to know exactly what you want to do, it's actually a good thing. If I was sure of what I wanted, I wouldn't have explored so many different possibilities, trying all kinds of things along the way. If I was focused on a specific destination and knew the steps I was going to take to get there, I would have been looking ahead with blinders on and not noticed all the other interesting possibilities that were just off to the sides.

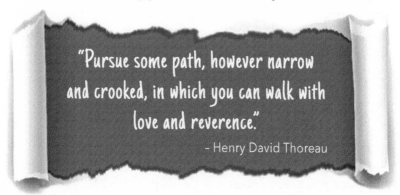

"Pursue some path, however narrow and crooked, in which you can walk with love and reverence."

- Henry David Thoreau

Keeping your mind open to the possibilities, even the ones you don't know exist, is something I think is very important in dog training and in life. I'm always telling my students that you should begin working with a dog using what you know and begin to take the necessary actions, but always be ready and willing to try new things and change your treatment plan along the way. It doesn't matter if most people train one way, if it's not working for you or you prefer a different technique, you need to try it. There is no definite, single path that is right. In the end, the best path won't be the one that someone chooses for you, but the one you decide upon for yourself.

In the beginning you're not going to have a clue as to what's the right direction to go in with your career. Just pick something that interests you and take action. Hopes, dreams and goals are useless without action. Any action - even the wrong action - is better than no action. Even if things don't work out (and they didn't many times for me) and you fall flat on your face (as I did over and over again), you'll learn something and be able to better adjust your course, or at least eliminate some choices. Whatever you do, don't let someone else pick up your game piece and put you on a path you know isn't right for you.

After I graduated from college, I started what would be a sixteen-year journey to figure out what I wanted to do when I grew up, encompassing five totally separate careers. I started out in graphic design, then switched to personal training, then over to software recruiter, then to real estate appraiser, until I finally landed on dog trainer. Sprinkled in there were some part time stints, including one handling reptiles and amphibians for a company that brought animals to schools and birthday parties.

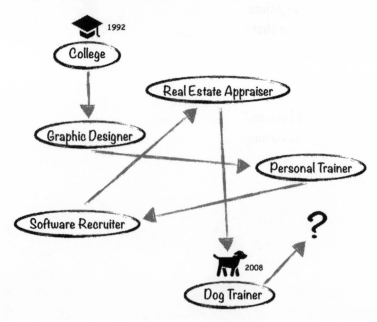

My path to finding dog training, which is what I feel is the job I was meant to do in life, wasn't really a straight line. In fact, you couldn't draw a more random, zig-zagged road map if you intentionally tried. It would have been nice if I could have figured it all out sooner and just cut to it right out of college, but I wasn't aware of it as an option back then. So, I just used the information I had at the time and picked a direction that I thought I would enjoy.

You don't have to have it all figured out now. You just need to pick a direction and go. Yes, you should do some research and make an educated decision before you jump into something important like a job choice. However, don't expect everything to align just right and be obvious. What no one really tells you (at least no one told me) is that you get to start over if it doesn't work out. You can decide at any time to stop, rethink your choice and decide to change it. Maybe that career you thought was great when you set off on it isn't what you expected or no longer makes you happy. If so, as soon as you realize this, start taking the steps to find a better option for you.

One thing I was really good at was recognizing when something I was doing was no longer enjoyable and getting out ASAP. I know too many people who are in jobs that don't make them happy but they stay there because it's just what they've always done. Then, after a period of years, it seems like an impossible task to switch and start over. You can definitely make a career change at any time. However, the longer you stay in something, the more daunting the idea of making a switch will become.

> "I have looked in the mirror every morning and asked myself: 'If today were the last day of my life, would I want to do what I am about to do today?' And whenever the answer has been 'No' for too many days in a row, I know I need to change something."
>
> - Steve Jobs

Only stay in a job as long as you're enjoying doing it. Life is WAY too short to spend it unhappy. Personally, I plan on squeezing the juice out of life. I want to enjoy every moment so I can look back in my old age and smile, instead of frowning in regret.

Making the choice to change your career path is actually kind of easy once you realize that you're not happy or completely fulfilled where you currently are. The hard part comes when you realize that you have to start at the beginning again. Starting at the bottom, learning new skills and struggling to work your way up to success is a very scary thing. And, the longer you've been at a job, the less appealing it will seem to go all the way back to the start again.

No, it's not easy. But it's worth it. I believe that nothing of real value comes easy, and the more you have to work for things, the greater the rewards are at the end. It will take guts, hard work and you're going to have to get out of your comfort zone, which can be frightening.

Know this, though. All the really great stuff in life is going to come to you by going out of your comfort zone. If you're not a little uncomfortable doing something, you're not pushing yourself enough. Staying within your comfort zone, doing only what you know is a rocket ship to a ho-hum life. And that sucks, so you're not allowed to stay there.

3

Looking Up
From The Bottom

"I think I want to be dog trainer," I said to my wife one cloudy afternoon in the summer of 2008.

My wife Michele looked at me with a slight head tilt. This wasn't something I had ever mentioned, so it kind of came out of left field. "Uh, okay," was all she could think of to say, both confused and concerned.

We had known I needed a new job for a few months, but I didn't know what I wanted to do. I considered going back to one of my previous careers in graphic design or personal training, but I knew those wouldn't make me happy. Since my real estate appraisal work had slowed, our income had dipped considerably and we were starting to feel the pressure. I needed to find a new job - and sooner rather than later.

I had a pretty much daily routine of checking online job websites, looking for anything I thought would be a good fit for me. For weeks I had scoured them, searching for my new dream job, but finding nothing that really interested me. My wife Michele is amazingly supportive in everything I've ever done. This is not an easy job given the fact that I'm prone to crazy ideas that make perfect sense to a guy like me who loves to take risks and acts without much thought, but her more sensible mind just can't process. Our slightly different thinking styles make us a nice, balanced couple. Without her being my voice of reason, I would have gotten into so many unnecessary jams. Yes, Michele is very supportive and understanding, but she does have her limits.

Time was passing by and our money was disappearing at an alarming rate. She was doing her part, working long hours in her job as a rock star ultrasound technologist, but we needed two incomes to survive. A few days prior, we had a slightly heated argument when she suggested that I might get a job at UPS delivering packages. She had said it was a good company (which I'm sure it is) that has good benefits (which they do), but I wouldn't hear any of it. Actually, it kind of offended me.

In my mind, there was no way I was going to settle and take a job that I was certain wouldn't make me happy. Don't get me wrong, there's nothing wrong with delivering packages for a living if that's what you really want to do. I just knew it wasn't for me, and taking a job just for the paycheck would be a prison sentence for me. So I went back to the online job boards. This particular day, while doing my usual, disappointing search and finding nothing remotely intriguing, something in the corner caught my eye: a short listing for a dog trainer.

Dog trainer, huh? I didn't even realize that was job. Sure, I went to training classes with my Pit Bull, Hayley, when I first adopted her a few years back but never thought much about it. As I pondered this discovery, I looked down at my dog who was at her usual post sleeping on the floor next to me.

I have a good relationship with my dog, I thought. However, I see other people not enjoying their dog as much as they could due to behavioral problems. What if I could help them achieve the same results that I had?

The more I thought about it, the more it made sense to me and the more excited I was by the idea. Since I was a kid, I've always loved animals. If you asked me at age ten what I wanted to be when I grew up, I would have said veterinarian, immediately. I voraciously read nature books and memorized all kinds of random animal facts (Did you know that the Wandering Albatross has the largest wingspan of any bird?) Then, as an adult, right after my job in a New York City advertising agency, I took a position at The Wildlife Conservation Society, located in the Bronx Zoo (a job I fought to get for almost a year). So animals were always near and dear to my heart.

Becoming a dog trainer definitely spoke to my soul, but was it also something that I could do well?

Sitting there, staring at the job listing, I gave it some thought and decided that it was something I could be good at it, maybe even really good. At this point in my life, I had jumped careers a number of times and always been able to become relatively successful every time, so why not this?

Actually, starting over and reinventing myself was kind of my thing. One of my good friends used to just shake her head and laugh every time we bumped into each other saying, "Every time I see you, you hand me a different business card." She couldn't comprehend how I could not only have a brand new job every time she saw me, but in an entirely different field, unrelated to anything I had ever done in the past.

I don't think taking the leap of faith down a totally unfamiliar career path is as hard for me as it is for other people because I love change. If you're a bit resistant to moving outside your usual life patterns, it can be more of a challenge to build up the nerve to do it. It's okay to feel that way, but don't let it stop you. You have to push through that. I love this old Henry Ford quote:

> "If you always do what you've always done, you'll always get what you've always got."

That pretty much sums it up for me. If you want your life to change, you have to change something (and sometimes everything). That means leaving what's familiar and breaking out of old patterns and habits because they are no longer serving you. If the thought of change makes you a little uncomfortable – that's a good thing! As we said, all growth happens outside of your comfort zone. If you're not feeling a little uncomfortable – like you're pushing yourself just outside the realm of what you think is possible – then you're not setting big enough goals and that means you're on the road to average (which we'll address a little later on in the book).

So, just like that, I decided to become a dog trainer.

I had zero experience and really no idea of what being a dog trainer was really like. However, the idea of it excited me. I thought, "What a cool way to make a living – helping both dogs and people." It's a win-win-win.

Now, I'm all for pushing yourself out of your comfort zone, taking a chance and going after your dreams, but I'm not reckless (most of the time.) Changing careers is not an impulse decision or something to jump into without understanding what you're getting into. That's why I immediately started doing some online research on how to become a dog trainer and what I could expect if I went for this new career.

After spending a few hours Googling my hands numb, I had looked through enough stuff to figure out that dog training looked like something I could do. I found resources that could educate me and saw that lots of people were already doing it, which is always a good sign. If others are successfully doing it, why not me? It's much riskier to go into a new market or be the first person to offer a particular service. If others are doing it, it means people are paying for it, so they might as well pay me for it.

Dog training sounded like something that I thought I would really enjoy, and because of that, I knew I could learn the necessary skills and do what it would take to make it work. That's the beauty of finding something you're passionate about doing – you're super motivated to make it successful because you're so happy and motivated to do it. So off I went.

There are two main ways to learn how to become a dog trainer: in person and online. Hands-on programs were where you travel to the organization and spend three to four weeks learning and working with dogs. Although hands-on learning is probably the best way to get an accurate understanding of the principals, this option has many drawbacks. Firstly, they are very expensive –

usually between $8,000 and $12,000, and I sure as hell didn't have that kind of money. Second, you have to be able to drop everything and fly out to their location for a few weeks, which was not an option for me.

The last big problem with in-person programs is that they cram an incredible amount of information into a short period of time and you're expected to remember and make sense of it all after you leave. Everything is thrown at you and there's no time to make sure you understand and really know how to implement it in the future.

For me, the negatives way outweighed the positives for this to be an appealing option. An online program, however, seemed to fit my lifestyle, needs and budget. There were a few options available but none that got me really fired up. I felt I needed some kind of foundation though. So after much deliberation, I chose the best of the few courses out there.

Upon completion of the course, I found myself disappointed with the education they provided and felt the amount of money they charged (about $3,500) was way overpriced for what was delivered. Their marketing info was outdated and they didn't really prepare me for building a business in today's economy. This poor experience is what fueled me to create the The FernDog Trainer Academy years later. I wanted to put together the exact course I wish I had when I was just starting out – a program that provided relevant information and resources, combined with the right assistance in setting up a successful, long term career.

Luckily for me, I had also been reading books on my own and seemed to have a natural ability working with dogs, so I wasn't slowed by the limiting content of the online program.

Starting a new business from the ground up is a challenging task – especially if you're doing it all by yourself. It takes a lot of hard work and there will be plenty of ups and downs that will test your resolve. The first few years building a new business can be an emotional tornado, leaving many people beaten and ready to throw in the towel - and I was no exception.

Within a few months of me deciding to pursue dog training, my wife became pregnant with twins. We had been trying to start a family for a while so it wasn't a complete surprise. My two daughters were born premature and required some extra attention and created quite a bit of extra expenses in the beginning. Honestly, I wasn't really psychologically, physically, emotionally or financially prepared to raise one child, let alone two. But like so much in life, you somehow figure things out along the way and make it work.

That's where we were in the first few years – in "making it work" mode. Looking back, it was one of the most challenging times of my life and I really have no idea how we were able to keep those two little people alive. Thankfully, my wife was there to continually save the day and stop me from doing stupid things (which I seemed to do in an almost predicable way).

It's funny how some moments in your life get burned into your memory so vividly that you can recall every single detail. About two years after I went all in on dog training and was hustling to grow my business, I had one of those emotionally memorable moments that would stay with me forever.

One day, when my kids were about a year and a half old, my wife asked me to run to the store to get some milk for the kids because we had just ran out. I got my sleep-deprived body moving, grabbed my keys and started to head out, but abruptly stopped halfway through the door, realizing something important. My wallet was empty.

Crap. I had no money. I stepped back in and quickly went over my options. We had no money in our bank account so the ATM machine couldn't help me, and after racking up some big credit card debt we had made a pact not to pay with plastic anymore until we were able to dig ourselves out. Double crap.

Standing in front of the closet by the door, I got an idea and went in and started going through all our jacket pockets, grabbing any loose change I could find. I went from coat to coat, grabbing anything resembling money and then sat down on the stairs facing the closet, counting my findings, praying it was enough to buy milk.

Suddenly I stopped and froze. The magnitude of the situation hit me like a punch to the gut. I felt weak and pathetic. In an instant I got an image of myself in my mind from above, sitting on the stairs counting pennies to scrape together enough to feed my kids. I don't think I've ever felt so pathetic and full of disrepair. The greatest fear of all married men is not being able to provide for our family, and it was glaringly obvious that I was failing mine big time.

I sat there at the bottom of my stairs, quiet and alone on the verge of tears, thinking that this has got to be one of the lowest points in my life. How the hell did I get to this point?

I asked myself, was I ever going to make any money as a dog trainer? Should I just forget the whole thing and just take any job I could get and start bringing money in? I only let the moment go on like this for about twenty seconds, then I made a choice. I decided that this moment did not define me. This moment was not going to make me compromise my goals. This moment was not going to poison me to throw away what I knew would make me happy. No way.

Yes, times were tough and I was down, but by no means out.

I wiped my damp eyes, counted out my change and went out and got milk for my family. I can still picture myself sitting on those stairs feeling hopeless, and I know there are plenty other people also sitting at the bottom, looking up at the stairway. I'm so glad I didn't give in to my doubts and negative feelings then. Looking back, I think it was one of the defining times in my life. I made a choice to fight for what I wanted in my life.

One day you're going to find yourself at the bottom of your stairs, feeling lost and defeated. At that time, you'll also be faced with the same choice. Will you just stay there at the bottom and give up or will you turn and climb your stairs again, one at a time?

If you do turn and climb, odds are you'll fall down them again, perhaps many times, as I have, but I want you to never dwell at the bottom for more than a moment or two. Stand up and go at it again. There's nothing for you at the bottom of your stairs but loose change. All the rewards in life are at the top and they are waiting for you.

So climb on.

4

Napoleon And
The Little Red Hen

I lifted my gaze from the pages and slowly lowered the book to my lap. My face was blank but my eyes sparkled as my mind absorbed what I had just discovered.

The sun was slicing through the trees and a soft breeze gently brushed against my face. The few dogs around me were all napping lazily in the midday afternoon, not paying me any attention. They had no idea that this moment would be one of those emotionally charged moments that would forever be burned in my memory.

I was in a small dog daycare where I worked part time as I tried to grow my new dog training business. The small building consisted of only one big room where small dogs, 35 lbs. and under, could hang out and play with their furry buddies while their human pet parents worked. It was a nice space and had some pretty nice amenities, including radiant floor heating and a huge painted mural along one wall. There was a sliding glass door that led to a small fenced-in patio where the dogs could relieve themselves and get some air. That's where I was on this quiet, seemingly uneventful day, sitting on a plastic white chair reading the book that would change the course of my life.

I was only about fifteen pages or so into the book when it hit me, and I remember looking up at that moment with the realization that what I had just read would change everything for me. It was so simple but was something that had never occurred to me. Reading it now, it made perfect sense and I could immediately see the mistakes of my past and how this knowledge would radically change everything for me moving forward.

> "There is a difference between wishing for a thing and being ready to receive it. No one is ready for a thing until he believes he can acquire it. The state of mind must be belief, not mere hope or wish. Open-mindedness is essential for belief. Closed minds do not inspire faith, courage or belief."
>
> - *Think and Grow Rich* by Napoleon Hill

After reading this, I now knew how to be successful - not only as a dog trainer - but in everything I did in life. My main problem for so long was not skill or lack of talent, it was my poor mental attitude and my lack of belief that had been holding me back from achieving everything I wanted. With this new information, there was nothing that could stop me and I was so upset with myself for not realizing this sooner. If I had, I would have been so much more successful in all the things I had tried and been way happier throughout my life.

I looked down at the book on my lap with tremendous gratitude, which quickly turned into a feeling of enlightenment. It was like I had been doing a jigsaw puzzle for such a long time and, although I had many of the pieces in place, I still had no idea what the image was. But now I found the key piece that revealed the picture and made the path to completion clear. It felt amazing.

Over the rest of the week I continued to study this book and discover the mistakes of my past that were stunting my progress, as well as the secrets used by some of the most successful people of all time. What really impressed me the most was that these were not some newly discovered principals but the proven formula used by countless people throughout time.

I'm not alone in being inspired by this one book. More than 100 million copies have been sold worldwide and even though the book was written way back in 1937, it still sells more copies every year. The reason? It's life changing information that is never outdated. This amazing book, that I now re-read every year or two, is *Think and Grow Rich* by Napoleon Hill. I HIGHLY recommend you give it a read or two (after you finish this equally epic book) and put its lessons into practice. It really is the roadmap to success.

The big take away I got, sitting in the dog daycare that day, was that my mindset was all wrong. Until that day I tended to be a glass is half empty kind of guy, who tended to concentrate on the negative instead of focusing on the positive outcomes that were possible. *Think and Grow Rich* changed that forever. In fact, reading this one book set me off on a journey of personal development that is still going strong almost a decade later. Previously, I had more of a victim mentality, tending to think my success, or lack of success, was due to external forces instead of my own doing.

Now I knew the truth - I was in control of my destiny. And it was liberating!

It turns out that we can steer our future and guide our outcomes - it's in our power. We're not mere observers in the game of life - we can control just about everything. I strongly believe that everything that has happened, is happening and will happen to you is 99% due to the choices that you make. Yes, there will be things you don't immediately control like a natural disaster, unexpected death in the family or a crash in the economy. However, how you think and act afterward is entirely under your power. You choose how you will respond to every event in your life.

This is energizing stuff because you can choose what you want to happen in your life.

It doesn't mean it's going to be easy though. In fact, it's likely to be pretty damn hard. But you can do it (whatever it is) if you make the conscious decision to do so. You can choose to not get depressed; you can choose not to dwell on failures; you can choose to get help; you can choose to do things differently; you can choose to not take it anymore; you can choose . . .

Some choices are easy, but the ones that will have the biggest impact on your life are no cake walk. They take a definitive choice followed by constant action, with a foundation of what Napoleon

Hill calls "definiteness of purpose." You need to have a burning desire to do what you chose. If not, you will give up at the first sign of difficulty.

This is where so many people fail. They get all fired up about a choice, they take action, it doesn't go as planned and they give up. I'll talk about failure a little later but I want you to know that obstacles are to be expected, but not accepted. If you want to, you can choose to find a way around them.

Choosing is not enough. Attitude is not enough. You have to be willing to put in the work and understand that things take time - almost always more time than you want or planned on. Once you make a choice to do something, you need to roll up your sleeves and work for it. The reason I've been able to become a successful dog trainer - starting from nothing and building up to a great business - is I was totally okay with working my butt off.

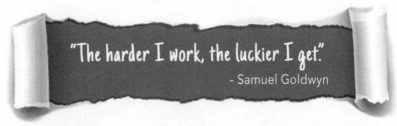

"The harder I work, the luckier I get."
- Samuel Goldwyn

I personally don't really believe in luck. I do believe in chance, but I consider that something different. Chance is something that happens randomly. People use luck very differently. They see luck as something that is caused to us, like there is someone or something deciding who gets "lucky" and who gets "unlucky". I don't buy that. I think there is nothing you can do about stuff that happens by chance, BUT you can affect how lucky you get by making the right choices and working hard. If you do that, it will seem that the odds are forever in your favor.

This is why you will never see me buy a lottery ticket. When you play the lottery, you are hoping that chance will magically send you a windfall with no work on your part. It's taking no responsibility for your future and just resigning to the fact that you're just a victim of whatever happens - you have no control. To me, any money spent on lottery tickets is wasted opportunity. It's not the money lost that makes me upset, it's the wasted mindset that's the killer. It means you've given up on making things happen for yourself. Your plan is blind hope. And that's not much of a plan at all.

I would much rather skip the poor odds of gambling and go for a sure thing; I bet on myself. Take the lottery money and spend it on education and personal development to better yourself. Buy a self-help book, take an online course or hire a life coach…whatever you want, just invest in bettering yourself and keep on doing it again and again. If you do that, you always come out a winner. Each book I read (and I read a lot), each podcast I listen to (and I go through a ton), each course I take (and I do some every year) and every coach/mentor I have (I'm never without one now) makes me a better person, better businessman, better husband, better friend, better dad and better human. I'm constantly improving myself in so many different ways and I can say it's one of the main reasons I've seen success (which I didn't see in the past when I didn't prioritize my personal and professional development).

Make the choice to improve and then take massive action.

Instead of sitting back and waiting for things to happen, you have to propel yourself forward, one step at a time. If that sounds like work, you're right, it is. When you see really successful people, it's not because they experienced a big windfall but because they worked like hell to get there. Don't be afraid of hard work, embrace it. Understand that it's part of the process and a sign you're going somewhere.

Okay, now that I've got you all fired up and ready to do the work, we have to talk about how you do the work. You have to put all your heart and soul into it. You can't just phone it in and do the minimum because your results will be in direct proportion to the quality of work you put in. My life has proven that if you try your hardest to do an awesome job - even when you're doing things you don't particularly like or believe are worthwhile - good things happen.

Looking back at the many jobs I've had over the last few decades, there have been some where I've given my all and others that I just didn't care enough about to do anything other than the bare minimum to get my paycheck. Good things came from some of them and nothing came of others. It's no surprise to me now that the jobs I gave my best effort to (even if I didn't particularly like what I was doing) resulted in some kind of good outcomes (aka luck). And the jobs I did halfheartedly didn't produce much of anything for me. Coincidence? I think not.

Always do your best, even if you don't think the job will have any future relevance. You never know what can happen and good things tend to happen to those who do good work. When I was working in a dog daycare for ten bucks an hour, picking up poop, I made sure I did the very best job I could do. I wanted to pick up poop better than anyone else there - I was the Poopmaster! Was it because I liked picking up poop? No, I'm not that kind of guy. Picking up poop day after day wasn't fun at all, neither was cleaning the play areas at the end of every day, but I did it as best I could - every day.

Doing a good job, day in and day out, was noticed by the owners of the daycare and I was able to build a great relationship with them, which led to all kinds of great things and opportunities.

Just last week I spoke at a conference here in New Jersey called Intergroom. It's a yearly event for dog groomers from all over the world and I spoke six times during the four days it ran. I've been doing a lot of speaking over the last year and have really fallen in love with it. Being in front of a live audience and sharing what I know is probably my all-time favorite thing to do. I love the energy of a live crowd and meeting new people. I've been slowly growing my speaking career, doing bigger venues and getting in front of larger crowds. Intergroom is one of the smaller conferences I've been invited to speak at, and this year, the average crowds in my presentations were about thirty to forty people.

I'm not going to lie, I love speaking to big crowds that are engaged and fill the room with energy. I feed off that and it makes delivering an exciting presentation easy. When you're in front of only a few people, it can be difficult to find that "umph" and get into it.

In one session at Intergroom this year, only three people showed up to my talk. That's it, three. There's nothing more depressing than standing in the front of a big room filled with a hundred chairs and seeing only three faces looking back. I was a little bummed out and had the wind taken out of my sails for a moment.

As the doors closed and I was about to start my presentation, I had a choice to make. I could let the lack of people showing up get me down and just whiz through my slides as quickly as possible, feeling defeated that no one came to see me (after all, it's not like a poor performance on my part was really going to hurt me with only three people to disappoint), or I could give these three people the very best I had.

Guess which I chose?

After a brief moment of disappointment, I shook it off and went all out in my usual animated and emotionally charged style. I moved around the room, jumped up and down as I told my stories and delivered the information with everything I had. Those three people got one of my best performances ever. Doing anything less than my best would have left me feeling empty and sent the few audience members home, wishing they skipped it like everyone else. Instead, they were smiling and thanked me for providing so much value.

One of the women in the "huge" crowd asked a question at the end, and in speaking with her, I discovered she lives in the same town as I do. Wow - what are the odds of that??? She's a new groomer in the area and liked what I had to say and has already started referring clients to me.

How awesome is that?

Always work like what you're doing could greatly impact your entire life, because you never know when it might.

Once again, if all this stuff sounds like a lot of work - you're right, it is!

In 2013, Ashton Kutcher won the Ultimate Choice Award at the Teen Choice Awards show. It might just be one of the best speeches I've ever heard. He said something there that everyone needs to hear. He said that, "Opportunity looks a lot like hard work." This is such a short, simple idea that most people overlook.

It reminds me of an awesome bedtime story I used to read my kids.

When my daughters were little, I would read them a bedtime story or two every night. It's probably one of my favorite Dad duties and I looked forward to it every night. We had a wide variety of books but the ones that I liked best were the books that contained a life lesson or positive message. After all, I want to do my best to teach my girls how to grow up to be independent, confident and caring people.

One night we read a book with a strong message that's super relevant for everyone, and I want to share it with you now because I think it can have a great impact on everything you do. The book I'm talking about is called *The Little Red Hen*. To my kids, it's a story about a hen and a bunch of other animals, but to me, it's the story of everyday life in our world.

One summer day The Little Red Hen finds a grain of wheat and decides it would be a good idea to plant it. She then asks all the other animals if they will help her, but every single one of them is too busy doing various leisurely activities. When the Little Red

Hen asks, they simple reply, "Not I!", and go back to their fun. So she says, "Then I will plant it myself." And then she does.

Soon the wheat grows and it comes time to reap it, and again our favorite rose-colored chicken asks the other animals if they will help her. A unanimous, "Not I!", comes back once again. At every new task, The Little Red Hen asks if anyone wants to help out and none of those lazy bums want to be bothered with it. Finally, our peppy poultry hero takes a scrum-diddly-icious loaf of bread out of the oven. She found the grain of wheat, planted it, reaped it, carried it to the mill, made it into flour, put it in the oven and now because of her hard work, The Little Red Hen has her yummy reward.

She then asks the other animals one final question, "Who will help me eat the bread?" Everyone immediately shouts, "I will!", and runs over, only to be shunned by The Little Red Hen who simply states, "No, I will eat it myself." And then she does – right in front of them.

The big question . . .

Who would you like to be in this story?

I see this fable played out repeatedly in real life (minus the animals wearing clothes). Too many people see someone enjoying the rewards of success and don't understand why they don't have similar success. When I meet another small business owner who's struggling and they look at me and say that I must be lucky or probably just know the right people, I feel a lot like The Little Red Hen.

I want to say to them, when I decided to become a dog trainer and worked for six months in a doggie daycare making $10/hour, learning dog communication and building an amazing relationship with the daycare owner, I asked, "Who will help me pick up the dog poop?" Those other trainers who decided that they didn't like cleaning up crap and making little money said, "Not I!"

When I spent countless days traveling from business to business cultivating relationships, giving seminars and talking to anyone I met, I asked, "Who will do free seminars and give away as much information as possible?" The other trainers said, "Not I!" And when I got business coaching I asked, "Who will pay for coaching to learn how to build a business that will last?" The answer was the same, "Not I!"

Success doesn't just happen by accident. You can't get there by sitting on your butt and hoping that things will just happen for you. There's no short cut, no magic pill and no easy button. Every success is forged by hard work and sacrifice.

If you don't want to spend the money, get up early, work late and miss out on some things, don't be surprised when you're left behind by those willing to do it.

How do you spend your down time? Are you watching TV and playing games on your phone, wasting valuable time that could be better used on education and to build yourself a better life? I'm actually writing this very sentence at 9:27 PM after a long day of working and taking care of my kids. Trust me, I would much rather be in the other room snuggled up to my wife watching Netflix, but I have big goals that I plan on reaching.

Please don't misunderstand me, I'm not saying to work around the clock and give up everything. Not at all. Rest and some downtime to switch off is imperative as well. You just need to get motivated, be willing to give up a few things and put in the time to make your dreams a reality. When there's someplace you want to go (business or personal goal), you'll need to get off the couch and start working at it.

If you want to sink your teeth into a mouthwatering piece of warm, homemade bread, you have to be willing to make a few sacrifices and work your tail feathers off.

5

Ratitude

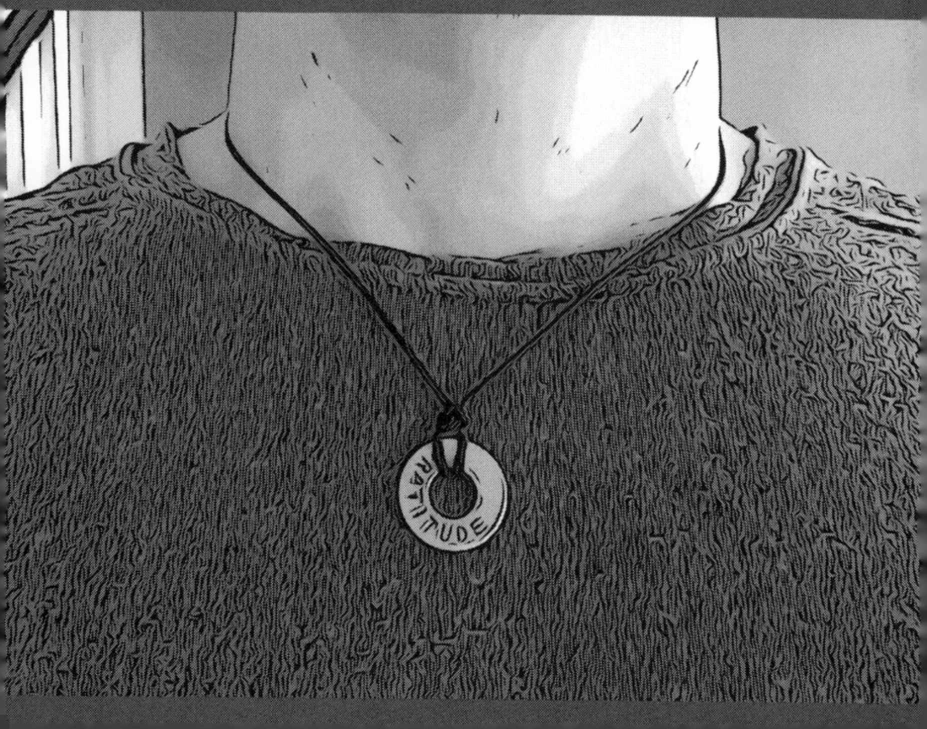
RATITUDE

At first, I never saw the dog bite me. I just felt the pain in my leg. I did, however, watch as he bit me a second, third and fourth time.

I was in Connecticut at a dog daycare and boarding facility where I was hired to do some consulting and staff training. After spending the morning speaking with the owner and management team, it was time to go into the daycare packs and work with the dog handlers.

We decided to start off in the big dog area where about fifty medium to large dogs romped. The facility had a pretty big indoor area with large garage doors that opened up into a nice sized outdoor yard. Even though today was cold - about 20 degrees Fahrenheit - the big doors were wide open and the dogs (seemingly oblivious to the brisk temperature) played both in and outside. I'm not a cold weather person at all - in all honesty, I'm a winter wimp - so I can't say I was happy to have to work in the cold for the next hour or so. However, the blustery cold weather did save me a trip to the emergency room that day.

I followed the owner of the daycare to the gate to the outdoor enclosure. As we reached the gate, all the dogs charged over, excited to see who was coming in. No matter how many times I do it, it's always a little unnerving entering a big pack and being rushed by dozens of big dogs. The owner of the facility walked in casually, with me following right behind.

The dogs ran right past her familiar figure and rushed over to see the more interesting new guy - me. Instantly, I was surrounded by dozens of excited dogs, making my progress into the yard impossible. I just stood there with my back against the gate I had just walked through, doing my best to ignore the dogs jumping up at me.

I was only in the yard for about five seconds when I felt the pain in my left shin. Immediately, I knew it was a bite (this was not my first rodeo). I looked down in time to see this thin, medium sized Border Collie mix wearing a jacket come darting back in and take another bite out of my other leg.

I gave out a little yell, trying to get the attention of the staff member who was working the yard nearby, but unaware of what was going on. I was hoping they could grab him and get him out of the pack. Unfortunately, they couldn't understand what I was saying because of all the canine chaos around me.

The little bastard darted in again and this time got me on the forearm. That was enough for me. Luckily I hadn't had time to move in and was still against the gate, so I just slipped back out of the yard, closing the gate behind me, without letting any of the dogs escape with me. I had been in the pack for no more than twenty seconds and took four bites from that same dog.

The owner moved over and asked what had happened. Over the noise of the dogs, I explained what had happened, pointed out my attacker to her and excused myself to the bathroom to assess the damages. It was in the bathroom that I discovered that winter had saved me. None of the bites really broke skin because of my jeans and big, heavy jacket. Had I not been wearing my winter coat or had I chosen dress pants, I would have had some pretty decent puncture wounds, requiring medical attention.

One of my early dog training mentors once told me, "Always wear jeans because they are like Kevlar and will save you from most bites." That advice has served me well and has in fact stopped me from getting bloody on more than a few occasions. If it had been summer, my naked arms would have had holes in them. Don't get me wrong, the spots where this guy tried to sink his teeth into me hurt and would later show some bruising, but it was pretty minor, thanks to my wardrobe.

I did my best to shake off the encounter, compose myself and left the safe confines of the bathroom. The daycare owner was waiting for me, concerned on how I was. I assured her that I was fine and that no real damage was done. She then informed me that they were told that the dog who came at me was reported by his owner to be fearful of men, however they never had any problems because they are a staff of all women. So it's not something they ever really think of or had any problems with.

With the troublemaker removed, I made my way back into the pack and spend the next hour there working with the staff on how to best manage and handle the dogs. The other dogs treated me well and there were no further incidents in the play group. I finished out my day of consulting with a brief summary with the facility owner. I thanked her for the opportunity to work with them and then headed out into the cold air to my car, where I now had an hour and a half commute back home to New Jersey.

It was 5:00 PM and the winter sun was setting, bringing the temperature down another ten degrees as evening started to descend. I started my car, let it warm up for a few minutes, typed my home address into my GPS app and headed out. I didn't even make it out of their parking lot when I could feel something was wrong with my car. I put it into park, got out, looked down at my passenger front tire and confirmed what I had feared - my tire was flat. Crap.

I left the car and walked back to the warm confines of the dog daycare where I called the AAA auto club, which I was a member of just for this kind of situation. After going through a series of annoying automated prompts, I was finally put on hold, left to tolerate a boring sample of annoying music that would remain stuck in my head for the rest of that week.

As I sat there waiting on hold, looking out at my immobile car as day faded into night, the daycare owner came out and asked what was wrong. I informed her that my car had a flat tire and she responded, "Wow, this is really NOT your day." First, I got bitten a few times by one of the dogs and now I get a flat tire, after hours, far away from home, on one of the coldest days of the year. I can see why some people might see that as bad luck. I saw things a bit differently though.

I looked at her with an honest smile on my face and said, "Not at all, I'm actually having a pretty great day."

I saw the situation quite differently than she did. I felt I was amazingly lucky. Yes, I did get bitten a few times by a dog, but none of those bites were serious because of my jeans and jacket. That was pretty lucky - they could have been much, much worse. Yes, my tire was flat and I'm far from home, but at least it happened here at the daycare and not when I was half way home, leaving me stuck on the side of the highway. I saw the whole situation as pretty fortuitous and was in very good spirits.

She looked at me a little surprised, but then she returned my smile and said, "That's a pretty good outlook."

Two people see the same exact situation but with two very different interpretations. She saw the misfortunes in my day, while I focused on the things that went right. I was able to take the negative events and locate the positives within them. That's what living with "Ratitude" is all about.

After waiting on hold for twenty minutes with AAA with no signs of human life on the other end, I noticed that there was an auto mechanic shop right next door. I quickly walked over and found them just closing up for the night. I explained my predicament and they agreed to take a look at my tire. Another lucky break!

They quickly noticed a nail in my tire that I must have run over on the ride up and patched it up for me in about ten minutes and only charged me $30. Very lucky indeed.

All in all, an outstanding day.

The term "ratitude" was inadvertently coined by one of my daughters and is now a part of our family's vocabulary.

Every night I tuck in my twin daughters before they drift off to sleep. It's one of my favorite things to do as a dad and something my girls always look forward to as well. One night a while back while I was leaning over my daughter, Jada, telling her how much I loved her and that I hoped she had a good night's sleep, she looked up at me quizzically and asked, "What's Ratitide?"

"What?", I replied, not knowing what she was talking about. I had never heard of such a word.

She reached up and gently took hold of the charm on my new necklace that I had just got earlier that day. It was so new that I had forgotten I even had it on. I had seen an ad online where you could get any word you wanted engraved into a silver ring of metal attached to a leather cord (www.myintent.org). The simple design combined with the ability to always have a special message with you really appealed to me. After some thought as to what one word I wanted attached to me day and night, reminding me of what is most important in my life, I decided on "gratitude."

Understanding and appreciating the many blessings all around me, each and every day, helps me take nothing for granted and keeps my focus on the good in my life. I really feel so lucky and happy to be living the life I am and am so grateful for everything; both the big, major parts of my life like my family, as well as the small, little details like having fresh drinking water, this computer I'm typing on right now, or even a nice cool breeze on a warm day.

Every single morning when I wake up, before I do anything, I have a moment of gratitude. I lie there in bed with my eyes closed and give thanks for everything I have in my life. I start my day with a feeling of prosperity and happiness that puts me on track to have an awesome day, no matter what may happen during it.

I highly recommend you try this practice. When you start the day grateful for what you have, your mindset for anything to come is colored with positivity. Having gratitude and taking time to reflect on it, even for just a moment each morning, is a superpower. It fortifies and energizes you, enabling you to realize how very lucky you are to be spending another day on Earth.

Gratitude is my most prized thing in life; it's one of the things responsible for turning me from a negative person into an upbeat, happy human being. It's what puts a smile on my face every day and what stops bad things from affecting me for too long. For all those reasons, it was the obvious choice for the one word to wear around my neck, every day.

> "I am happy because I'm grateful. I choose to be grateful. That gratitude allows me to be happy."
> - Will Arnett

When Jada noticed it around my neck, the pendant had shifted and moved slightly so that the leather cord covered the "G," leaving it simply saying, "RATITUDE".

I quickly realized what had happened, but decided I liked the word Ratitude, so I decided to run with it. I told my girls that Ratitude is more than just being grateful. It starts with that, but is then mixed with positive thinking, finished with a splash of exuberance - a playful zest for life.

Gratitude + Positivity + Excitement = Ratitude

Now my girls and I try to live our lives with constant Ratitude.

I would define Ratitude as the feeling of gratitude mixed with a healthy dose of positivity. This is not something that has come easily for me, and definitely not the attitude I had earlier in life. It's something I've had to work at over the last decade to cultivate. Those two qualities, being grateful for everything and looking at the bright side of life, are the keys to living a happy, more fulfilling life. They will help you appreciate ordinary, trivial occurrences as well as to not dwell on unfortunate events for more than a moment.

They say that life is not what happens to you, it's how you react to it all. This is way more than just positive thinking - it's changing your reference point of your life. Once you make Ratitude your anchor, you're able to steer your thoughts to a better, more productive and happier perspective. Yes, stuff will happen and occasionally the shit will hit the fan, but instead of sinking into a pool of negativity and depression, you can rebound quickly by looking at the big picture and appreciating the blessings all around you.

Ratitude is something that's available to all of us. It's a skill that can be learned and a habit that can become second nature. If you're a negative thinker, as I used to be, it will take some time and conditioning to change your default thought process. However, with time, it can become an amazing tool that brightens all the moments of your life.

The consequences of not living with Ratitude can be quite severe. During my teens, twenties and early thirties, I was a bit of a downer, to say the least. I remember owning a plain black t-shirt in college that simply said, "Leave me alone, I'm depressed."

That makes me so sad now and I so wish I could get into a time machine and find that ignorant and misguided young Fern and smack some sense into him. I would tell him how much he was missing out on because of his attitude. I would explain that he could have much greater success and happiness in ALL areas of his life if he just changed his attitude.

At the time, I just didn't see it and had no one to help me understand a new (and more truthful) perspective. Now, I can look back and see that so much of my time was wasted with a poor experience due to my poor outlook on my life. I had no gratitude - even though I had so much to be thankful for. In fact, I had every reason to be happy and upbeat, but I just couldn't see past my own disillusioned viewpoint.

Just by shifting my perspective, I could have enjoyed those days so much more. Don't let that happen to you. I don't want you to waste even one more day living life less than you can. Practice Ratitude every single day - make it part of your routine and weave it into your lifestyle. If you do that, you will create a smile on your face that can't be brought down by life's trivial curveballs. Bad situations will be minimized, the "normal" aspects of life will seem sweeter and the good stuff that happens to you will level up to amazing.

The jobs I had, the relationships I was involved in and the experiences I had could have all been improved if I just had a better attitude and appreciated the simple gifts all around me. I severely hampered my happiness by not realizing this sooner. I can't get those years back - they're gone for good. I can't change the past, but my days since making the shift have been amazing.

You get to choose the brush you paint the story of your life with - it's 100% up to you. Paint them with a grey color and your life will be dark, choose a bright pallet and watch your world become vibrant and fun.

With Ratitude you'll be able to reach new levels of personal success and happiness that were previously believed by you to be out of reach. This is not just self-help, rah-rah BS - it's been documented in numerous scientific studies. It made all the difference for me and I strongly believe it can do the same for you.

Live every day with Ratitude, my friend.

6

Yeah! Vacation's Over

I was walking on the beach with my wife and kids on an overcast July afternoon. The cloud cover hadn't damped our mood as we searched for shells, chased each other at the water's edge and made a valiant attempt at getting a kite into the air. My twin girls were laughing as my wife and I walked hand in hand, soaking in the last day of our summer vacation.

My wife mentioned a few times how she hated to have to leave and wished we could just stay for another few days. I nodded in quiet agreement, but was inwardly smiling at the prospect of heading back home. I had also had an awesome time on our beach vacation but, unlike my wife, I couldn't wait to get home because my job was not just work - it was my passion and I loved it.

The feeling of contentment in knowing that I would soon be back to my "daily grind" kept my spirits high and helped me really enjoy the last night on vacation with my family. When you don't like what you do for a living, the weight of the realization that you'll soon be forced to return to the dreaded J-O-B sits in the back of your mind and taints your present experiences. Translation: it bums you out.

I've felt that way in the past, so I had sympathy for my wife, who likes her work, but it's not something that gets her excited to jump out of bed and go do. It's definitely a job, and if they weren't paying her decent money to do it, there's no way she would do it. I know that feeling - I've been there in some of my past career choices - not anymore though.

To me it seems that most of the people out there are not all that thrilled when Monday morning rolls around. In fact, a recent Gallup poll found that 85% of people worldwide dislike their jobs. 85% - that's crazy! Although you might feel a little better knowing that you're not alone in feeling unsatisfied at work, it needs to be a big slap in the face that things need to change. You'll see why when we do the math (I know I told you my math skills suck but this is easy math even I can do).

We all get the same 24 hours each day. Assuming that we sleep 8 hours a night, that leaves us 16 waking hours to do stuff.

24 hours a day - 8 hours of sleep = 16 hours of waking time.

The average person spends about 8 hours a day at work, equating to a 40-hour work week. I know plenty of people who are working much more than that, but we'll go with 8 hours a day for this example. That 8 hours per day spent at work is half of our waking time each day.

16 waking hours a day - 8 hours of work = 8 hours left do what we want.

That means that about half of our waking lives is spent at work. If you don't like your job that means that you're spending about HALF OF YOUR LIFE UNHAPPY.

Take a moment and let that sink in.

If you don't like your job, 50% of your life sucks. Is that how you want to live your life???

We only get one shot at this, you know. There are no do-overs. This is your one and only life, so it would make sense to make the absolute most of it and enjoy your time here as much as you can.

Personally, I plan on squeezing the juice out of life, which just means I want to create as much happiness as I can each and every day because I'm not going to get a moment back. I want to live life to the fullest and that means enjoying not just 8 of my waking hours, but as close to 16 as I can muster.

Sounds like a good plan - but there is a problem. We've been told that work is something you have to do to survive in this world and you just have to find something practical that will pay your bills. If you subscribe to that propaganda, you'll end up one of the many people who stare at the clock all week, counting down the seconds until Friday night. Then, you'll get a feeling of dread in your stomach around 4:00PM on Sunday as the realization sets in that the weekend is almost over and you will soon have to return back to work.

That's no way to live, is it? Plodding through five days of work, just for two measly days of fun at the end of the week - who decided this was the way life should be?

I invite you to challenge the notion that you can enjoy those five days in between weekends. You can choose work that gets you fired up and excited to go to every day. I know, because I'm living it.

Too many people choose their career based on what they think will make them the most money instead of what will bring them the most fulfillment. They make a "sensible" choice based on what they believe will bring stability, financial freedom and security. Now, those things are not bad, in fact they are all important. You should definitely factor in those variables, but they shouldn't be your main motivation in choosing a career that you could be doing long-term.

Let's say I was single, and I came to you and said I was getting married. You would say, "That's so exciting, tell me about your future wife." If I then told you she's very stable, has a lot of money and will stay with me for a long while, what would you think? If that was my main motivation for choosing this woman to spend the rest of my life with would you think it was a smart decision? Hell no!

Yes, those things are important, but if that was how I chose her to be my wife I would be miserable before we returned from the honeymoon. You should pick a partner who you really enjoy being with; someone who makes you light up every single day and that you love with all your heart. Why? Because you're going to spend the rest of your life with them and if you're not passionate about the relationship, you will be unhappy 'til death do you part.

Stability, financial freedom and security are important, but if they come without passion, you will have to pay a big price. Your career is like another partner in your life and you need to go into it like a marriage. Do you take this career to have and hold from this day forward, for better or for worse, for Monday and for Friday, in sick days and in overtime, 'til death do you part?

If your career were a person, would you marry them?

I know all this because I've been suckered into being "practical" and "smart," and learned the hard way. I was once tempted by the sweet lure of a career that paid lots of money and would give me everything I thought I needed and wanted (spoiler: I was wrong on both accounts).

In 2003, I was a personal trainer and sports nutritionist helping adults get in better shape and become healthier. I worked in an upscale gym and worked with my clients one-on-one. It was a lot of fun and I truly enjoyed helping people improve their bodies and minds. Then, one day I decided that I needed to make more money. Although I could have stayed in the fitness industry and pursued a management position and worked my way up, I was a little burned out at the hours I was working and felt that would take me away from the clients, which is what I really enjoyed about the job.

Hearing my plight, a friend of mine offered me a job at his company as a recruiter for high-level software salespeople. He told me that I could make a boat load of money doing it and that he would teach me everything I needed to know. I immediately started daydreaming about all those dollar signs and how awesome my lifestyle would become. I was sold and I told him I was in.

For many people making a complete career change, moving to something you know absolutely nothing about can be quite stressful, but I wasn't too worried. After all, this was not the first time I've switched careers and I really love change; change is exciting, with new possibilities and opportunities. The fear of change and the unknown can paralyze some, keeping them from trying new things, exploring new ideas and preventing them from becoming more than what they already are. I know it can be scary taking chances and leaving what's familiar - even if you know it's not the right thing for you.

It's okay to be afraid and unsure - just don't let it stop you from going for what you want. If you just stay in your comfort zone, you'll greatly limit your life and never realize your full potential. Everything great in this world resides somewhere on the other side of your comfort zone.

People who accomplish great things and have amazing lives don't stay in their comfort zone. They, like you, feel the fear of the unknown but they don't allow it to stop them. They move forward in the face of fear. I'm not telling you to take unnecessary or stupid risks for the sake of "going for it." No way. You want to take calculated risks. That means you've done some investigation on what you're about to do and you have some information leading you to believe that this could be a beneficial thing for you. You don't have all the answers and the deck may still be stacked against you. However, you see the positive outcome possibilities.

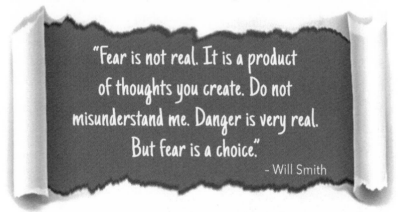

"Fear is not real. It is a product of thoughts you create. Do not misunderstand me. Danger is very real. But fear is a choice."
- Will Smith

Although becoming a software sales recruiter was something I never did, my friend promised to teach me anything I needed to know, and I knew I would work hard to become successful. That combined with the lure of a big payday was enough for me to jump into the unknown and see where it would take me.

My fatal flaw - one that I would never allow myself to make again - was that I didn't like sales or care at all about computer software companies, let alone recruiting. I showed up for work, sat down in my cubical and dove into it. I read through countless trade magazines, followed my friend's instructions and listened intently to the three other recruiters seated beside me. The learning curve was a little tough with so much techno-jargon and industry specific knowledge to soak up, but after a few weeks, I started to get a sense of what I was supposed to do.

Soon I was cold calling my day away and came to the realization that this kind of sales really sucks. It's not that I didn't like - I HATED it. I was expected to make 50 - 100 calls a day and the two partners were keeping score and had no problem letting you know when you were slacking. The days dragged by and I found myself doing something I had never really done before - I continually counted down every second until Friday evening and then dreaded the coming of Monday morning.

Just as I was getting fed up and on the edge of sanity, something happened. I closed a deal.

As a recruiter, when you place someone at a company, you get a commission based on a percentage of their salary. I don't remember how much money that guy was hired for but I do recall the huge check I got because of it. It was more money than I have ever gotten in one lump sum. I was so happy and, like a druggie, I was hooked again and after a weekend celebrating and spending, I showed up Monday morning with renewed vigor.

Soon I closed another deal, and another. Within a few months I had made more money than I had the prior year as a personal trainer. I bought new furniture and went on a tropical vacation and spent my money with glee. Then, unexpectedly, mainly due to luck and being in the right place at the right time, I closed the biggest deal in the company's history. This brought me an insane bonus check and helped me meet my yearly sales quota a full four months before the end of the year. I was living the dream. I had more than enough money, was living the VIP lifestyle and I was only just getting started in this field.

The only problem was I was miserable.

All that money and success had not changed my dislike for the work or my lack of passion for the subject matter. Direct sales is not an easy job and it was getting very clear that I was not cut out for it.

Since I had already hit my sales goals and had plenty of money, I started slowing down on my calls and not doing really much at all while at work. This pissed off the one partner (not my friend, the other one) and he started getting on my case to "dial, dial, dial!" I explained that I had already hit the goals that he had set for me and now I could do what I wanted. He didn't care. Every time I made money, so did he. The partners got a cut of every deal I closed, so the more I brought in, the more money they would make too.

Reluctantly, I started back up again. As the year's end approached, my misery was at an all-time high. I became depressed and a bit belligerent at the partners (I found out much later that my fellow recruiters had a pool as to when I would finally lose it and take a swing at one or both of the partners).

The final straw came one day when I was trying really hard to find this one guy a job. I had been speaking with him for about a month and, so far, couldn't find him anything good. The reason I couldn't place him was because he was not really qualified for the positions that I typically filled. Normally I wouldn't have spent so much time on him, but he seemed like such a nice guy and he needed to find a job soon.

He called me every other day, asking if I had anything for him, sounding more desperate each time. He told me that he was in financial trouble due to being out of work so long; he was laid off and the bills were piling up and his family needed him to get back to work.

His situation was dire and I felt so badly for him. I really wanted to find something for him, so I spent much of my days looking for new leads and trying to find him someone who would give him an interview. Then one day, the other partner (not my friend) came over to see what I was working on.

He took one look at the guy's resume and said, "Why the hell are you wasting all your time on this shithead?" I explained that he was in bad shape and really needed a job and I was doing my best to help him. He told me again that he was a "shithead" and to let him go and focus on "A" players.

That was the last straw for me. I felt horrible and knew I had to get out as soon as I could. This was not the kind of person I was and this was not the kind of work I wanted to do - no matter how big the paycheck.

It was the middle of the holiday season and work was slow so I decided to stick it out until the end of the year. As luck would have it, a client from the gym I used to work at was looking for some real estate appraisers. I knew nothing about it and it would be a big pay cut, but I would have taken just about anything to get out of recruiting. So I took the job and would start in the new year.

Although I had planned on quitting after New Year's, I couldn't wait. I was at a New Year's Eve party with my friend who got me the recruiter job and I quit just before the stroke of midnight. For the first time since starting work as a software recruiter a year ago, I felt truly happy.

Lesson learned: money does NOT equate to happiness.

Little did I know, I was just about to start a job that was even more dangerous to my happiness.

7

Comfortably Unhappy

It was the day after Christmas and I was relaxing at home with my family when I heard my wife call my name. She was standing at our front door, urgently gesturing me to hurry over to her. I hustled over and looked out at the street below. My house is set up on a hill along a busy street in Bloomfield, New Jersey, where cars zoom past at speeds well over the 25 MPH speed limit. However, on this day, no one was going very fast due to the accumulating snowfall and the medium-sized dog that was walking in the middle of the road.

I quickly threw on my coat, grabbed a slip leash and headed out into the late afternoon snow. The dog was literally walking in the middle of the street followed by some impatient drivers and a few people on foot who were trying to coax it out of the road. As a few of the Good Samaritans drew near, the dog broke into a light jog and veered off the road and onto the sidewalk.

As I approached, I could see that the dog was a light brown female, older Chow mix with a little stump for a tail, and a rather confused look on her face. I wasn't sure if it was in shock or just a little disoriented. Although she showed no signs of fear or anxiety, she was a bit wary of the humans closing in.

One woman tried to coax it over with some dog biscuits, while another person knelt down and tried to verbally lure the dog in. Neither approach worked, and the dog turned and jogged toward the back of one of the homes lining the street.

The wind picked up and the snow began to fall at a more rapid rate. As I reached the back of the yard, I realized it was just me and one other guy left in the chase. I felt the dog was unsure but not in any way aggressive or fearful, and that I just needed to gain her trust slowly.

Behind the homes there was a small wooded area containing a small brook. The snow-covered dog ran into the tree line and moved along the water's edge for about twenty feet, then stopped and looked back at us. I turned my back to her and started walking backwards toward her. The other guy with me saw this and asked if I had done this before. I explained that I was a dog trainer and that I was trying to make the dog as comfortable with my presence as possible.

I don't know if it was his confidence in my ability or the cold of the wind, but the next time I looked up, he was gone, leaving me alone with the dog. I knew this was actually a good thing because too many people would only frighten this timid girl off.

She went deeper into the woods and I slowly followed. After a time, she came to a section of fallen trees that left her kind of trapped in a dead end. The only way out, besides coming back toward me, was a small path that lead back to the houses on my street. I carefully crept forward, inch by inch. When I got about ten feet from her, she started to walk reluctantly toward me. It seemed like she was going to risk going past me to gain her freedom. I got my leash ready, knowing I may only get once chance at catching her.

When she got within arm's reach, I spoke to her softly and gently tried to place the loop of my slip leash over her head. I couldn't get it around her neck and she bolted backward. That's when she noticed the path leading back up to the houses and went for it.

My heart sank, thinking that I just blew my one and only chance to catch her. She ran up the narrow path and I followed, refusing to give up. She reached another house and started walking around one side. I sprinted around the other side of the house hoping to cut her off before she reached the street again. It worked, and I came around the corner just as she reached the two cars parked in the driveway.

We played a little game of cat and mouse around the cars, trying to out maneuver each other, but at last she hesitated a little too long and I was able to slide the leash around her neck. The feeling of relief and triumph was overwhelming.

I arrived back at my house with my reluctant companion forty-five minutes after I had set out. During that time, another inch or two of snow had hit the ground, and the darkening sky showed little signs of slowing. I called animal control, knowing that the odds of getting anyone out here in this weather was slim, but to my surprise, the dedicated animal control officer arrived at my house just fifteen minutes after I hung up the phone.

When I thanked Dan, the animal control officer, for coming out in such bad weather, he simply said, "No problem, that's what I do," and his smile revealed just how much he really cared for the animals under his care.

That night, a blizzard covered Northern New Jersey, blanketing the landscape with two feet of snow and gusty winds. I don't think there is any way a stray, old, disoriented dog would have survived the night in those elements unprotected.

Later that night as I was cozily lying in my bed, and the little stray dog was warming up at the Bloomfield Animal Shelter, I thought about what had just happened. That little dog spent who knows how long out on the streets trying to elude capture, and when she was finally leashed up by this strange human and taken into captivity, it must have seemed like such bad luck to her. She had failed – I captured and incarcerated her against her will – certainly a horrible event.

However, when you consider the winter blizzard that would have probably killed her had she remained outside, and that her human family came the very next day to take her back home, getting leashed and locked up was the best thing that ever happened to her.

What she thought was the worst possible outcome at the time, turned out to be a tremendous blessing once you discover the big picture. When faced with negative events in your life, remember that given some perspective, you may feel very differently about the situation.

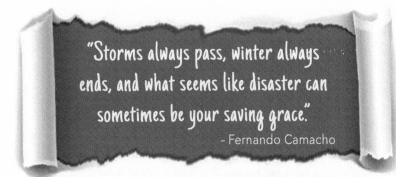

"Storms always pass, winter always ends, and what seems like disaster can sometimes be your saving grace."
— Fernando Camacho

Looking back now, I see how one of the seemingly worst times for me turned out to be one of the big positive turning points of my life. I didn't know it at the time, but being a real estate appraiser put me in grave danger, not because of any kind of physical perils, but what it could do for my long-term happiness.

The most dangerous career you can have is one that you don't mind that much. If that's how you describe it, you're in trouble. If your job is okay, or not bad, or you find yourself saying things like, "it's a living," or "another day another dollar," or "back to the grind," you need to think about making a change.

One of the longest runs I had in a career before I found dog training was as a real estate appraiser, and that's exactly how I felt about the work. The best way I can describe it is that I was comfortably unhappy. Didn't hate it, but definitely didn't love it either. Unlike my time as a recruiter, there was nothing I could identify as dissatisfying, but there wasn't something I was in any way passionate about. Although I didn't love it, there was nothing strong enough driving me to make a change.

If you're not sure if you're currently in danger of this happening to you, a good test is how you feel about talking about what you do for a living. When you're out at a social gathering and someone asks you what you do for work, do you just give them a quick unemotional reply or are you excited to discuss it? If you don't say much or don't really care to talk about it, you may be in the danger zone.

Comfortably unhappy is why people stay in jobs that they're not at all excited about, feeling unfulfilled for years. The only way people get out of these types of careers is by an outside force. They get unexpectedly laid off, the company goes under or, in my case, the economy crashes.

In 2008, the United States experienced the worst economy since The Great Depression. Seemingly overnight, there was no more work for a real estate appraiser and I had to figure out what I was going to do to make money - and quick. At the time, it seemed like just about the worst thing that could happen to me. I was newly married and we were trying to start a family, and out of nowhere, my income was gone.

There are so many success stories that begin with events that appear to be horrible misfortunes. However, as time goes by, you realize they were the best thing to happen because they forced the person to make a change that they would never have made on their own - and those changes led to some amazing things. That's why having my appraising work dry up was the best thing to happen to me (although it definitely didn't seem like it at the time).

Please don't wait for some unforeseen external event to make a change in your life that you know you need to make now. Allow me to be the kick in the ass to snap you out of your complacency.

Otherwise, you'll be stuck with a ho-hum job until your dying days. That sucks - big time. No one wants that, but that's what so many people unnecessarily settle for.

I'm not going to let that happen to you though – not on my watch! You're not going to be one of those people with regrets later in life. No way, my friend. Take the time and the action to figure out what gets you fired up and head in that direction sooner rather than later.

> "All your dreams can come true, if you have the courage to pursue them."
>
> - Walt Disney

You must beware the drift of life. If you just keep your head down, do your work and not think about if you really like it, you might just pick your head up one day and realize a whole bunch of years have gone by (time you will never get back). If you're not aware, time can fly by, leaving you much further down a road you don't really want to be on. And the farther you drift, the harder it is to find a way back.

The good news is that your life is not left to the whim of the currents. It's 100% under your control. You get to choose what you do and what you decide not to do. You get to pick your path. If you don't like it, you get to choose to leave it and find another. Too many people have a victim mentality, where they blame their circumstances on external forces. They say their life is where it is because of the economy, the government, their parents, their education (or lack of), their financial situation, their husband, wife, kids, the weather, and on and on and on . . .

All of that is NOT why you are where you are today.

Remember, there's only one reason why you're at where you're at in your life, and that is because of your choices. That's it. YES, we're back on choices again. I know we already discussed it a little earlier, but it's so critical you understand this.

Realizing that I was in control of where my life could go was a game-changer for me.

Understanding you have the power to guide your life is an amazingly powerful thing. You are moving yourself in some direction based on your choices, so make sure you're heading in the direction you want.

Embrace this knowledge and be very deliberate and calculated with your choices. Even seemingly trivial decisions can have big repercussions on your future.

Choosing to sit on the couch tonight and watch TV instead of researching new job opportunities is a choice that will delay your dream life. Choosing to eat that greasy burger instead of healthy salad is a choice that can lead to a habit of unhealthy eating.

Little choices can add up quickly.

Everything is a choice and the choice is yours. Make sure your choices are serving you and get excited that you have the option to choose. The sooner you take responsibility for your life, the sooner your life will improve.

The good life awaits, if you choose to go after it.

8

All Skills Are Learnable

"No, we don't have the money," my wife told me.

I can't say the response surprised me. In fact, that's what I expected her to say because it was indeed the truth. We didn't have the money to spend on much of anything - let alone some unknown online course from some stranger on the internet. My wife's concerns were valid. We were strapped for cash so why would I even consider spending $1,000 on something that she didn't understand and that could very well be a scam?

I spent the last couple of years growing my dog training business on the side while being a stay at home dad for my twin girls, who were about three years old at the time. Dog training was going well. However, the challenge of juggling my work with taking care of my girls was proving to be very difficult.

The breaking point came when one of my daughters got a nasty cold and had to stay home from daycare for two weeks. As soon as she got better and was able to return to daycare, my other daughter got sick, causing her to stay home for two weeks. Then when I finally got her healthy and back to daycare, I got sick and was laid out for two weeks. If we do the math, that makes six weeks that I had to be home and couldn't work. When I don't work, I can't make money, which kind of sucks - a lot.

After that, I came to the realization that we couldn't continue like this. With little kids continually getting sick (you parents feel my pain), I knew that there were more long days at home to come for me, prohibiting me from doing my work as a dog trainer. I had to figure out another way to bring in some money that didn't require me leaving my house, something I could do on my time, even while a cranky baby or two yelled in the background.

Lucky for me, we live in the most abundant time of opportunity in human history, all thanks to this little thing called the internet. I'm old enough to remember a time when there was no World Wide Web, which is hard to imagine now that we're connected to the entire planet via a small rectangle in our pocket. I'm not sure what I would have done if I didn't have access to the magic of the internet and all the opportunities it connected me with. But who cares, I did have it and I was going to use it to make some money for my family.

After doing some research, I decided that I could create an online course and take my dog training knowledge global by leveraging the power of the internet. I could then work and (hopefully) make money while staying home with my girls. I knew it was the only way we were going to be able to survive in our current situation. The problem was that I had no idea how to create an online course, let alone how to market and then sell the thing. I had confidence I could do it, if I just could find someone to show me how.

That's how I came across this guy named Chris Farrell, an online marketing guru who just came out with a new program called "Chris Mentor Me". It was a group coaching program that would consist of live training on how to build an online course from scratch over the course of about six weeks. I had never heard of Chris Farrell, but the program seemed to be exactly what I needed to learn how to get my online course built. The only problem was the money. A thousand bucks is a lot of money and we needed every penny to attempt to pay our bills. This combined with not knowing if it was legit, understandably made my wife more than a bit nervous.

Not me though - I was confident because I believe in the power of education. I knew that we weren't losing money here, we were investing it. I had a feeling that the knowledge I would gain would be valuable long after the cash was gone - even if I wasn't successful in creating this online course. After much debate (and many promises of a big upside by me), we finally agreed that I would take the course and put the $1,000 on our already over-extended credit card.

As soon as the class began, I dove in 100%. I followed every instruction to the letter, watched every video (multiple times), took part in all the live calls and did the homework. Immediately, I saw how quickly my learning curve shortened and I got so much further, so much faster, than I could have ever gotten on my own without the course. My teacher, Chris Farrell, proved to be a man of his word and really over delivered on the content of the course. One thing he kept saying to us, over and over again was . . .

"All skills are learnable."

It's so true.. just about anything you want to do, you can do, if you just learn how to do it. We often think some skill sets are just out of our reach, or that others are just "born with that talent". Although talent does account for some levels of achievement, just about anyone can learn how to do the basics - enough to get them by. All you need to do is find someone to teach you. If you have the desire and put in the work, all skills are learnable.

I have come back to that quote many times in my life. Whenever I want to do something I'm not sure how to do or am embarking on a new challenge (or career), I remind myself that "all skills are learnable". If others can do it, so can I.

One great example of this came for me in December of 2013, a couple of years after I completed the *Chris Mentor Me* course. I had seen a bunch of people selling t-shirts online via Facebook ads and it really intrigued me. As an ex-graphic designer and a big wearer of t-shirts, the idea of creating my own shirts and then getting paid for it sounded pretty good.

My priority was still being there for my girls and, although I had been experimenting with the online courses, I could still use some extra income in addition to my part-time dog training. T-shirts would be a great creative outlet and the companies that produced them made it easy by only printing each shirt upon purchase, so I didn't have to put any money out up front. So I decided to give it a go. I created my first shirt, whipped up some ads on Facebook and waited for the money to start rolling in.

Nothing happened.

Well, not completely nothing. I did sell a few shirts, but nothing like all these other guys were doing and my ad spend was more than I was making, so I was losing money. This was not quite the way I envisioned it happening. Deep down, I knew it wasn't my designs, but my Facebook ad strategy. I really had no idea what I was doing with it. Running ads on Facebook is a complicated thing and not something you can just wing.

After two shirt campaigns, I had lost a couple hundred dollars. Discouraged, I thought to myself, "Oh well, I guess I'm just a big dummy and can't figure out this Facebook ad thing," and I gave up.

All that week I couldn't sleep. I couldn't let it go. If all these other guys were able to figure Facebook ads out and have so many profitable t-shirt campaigns, I should be able to do it too. I mean, I'm a fairly smart guy, right?

Then I remembered, "All skills are learnable."

I thought about it a little more, and then it hit me. I didn't fail because I couldn't do it, I failed because I didn't know how to do it. All I needed to do was to track down one of the people who was currently doing it successfully and get them to teach me how to do it. I dove into the internet and began searching. In no time I found a course that detailed exactly what I wanted to do; sell t-shirts online via Facebook ads. Perfect!

I purchased the course for $97, implemented what they taught and BAM - success. As soon as I figured out how to do it the right way, it was easy. I was amazed. I went from losing money on my t-shirt campaigns to making a few thousand dollars in a few days. Imagine if I just accepted my early failure and gave up. I would have missed out on an amazing opportunity and a whole lot of much needed money. The course was good, but it was pretty basic and I knew this was only the tip of iceberg as to what was possible. I knew there was more I could do with this revenue stream and wanted to expand on what I was doing to take it to the next level.

Back to the internet I went to find someone that could help me up my game - and this one guy kept coming up in my searches. His name was Trey Lewellen and he was making a killing selling t-shirts on Facebook. I reached out to him and, as luck would have it, he had a coaching program teaching everything I wanted to know. I guess it's true what they say, when the student is ready, the teacher appears.

There was only one problem - and it was a big one. The coaching program cost $1,000 per month! I was pretty bummed. There was no way I could afford that.

Trey was pretty confident in what he taught and assured me that I would make all that money back and more by the first month. I knew I could make selling stuff online work and I was pretty sure Trey could teach me how to do it, so I was in, but with one small obstacle to overcome. I had to convince my wife once again to spend money we didn't have - and this time it wasn't $1,000 one time, it was $1,000 every month. Gulp.

To be honest, I really don't remember how I was able to convince her to let me go ahead with it. I think she's just awesome and unbelievably supportive. Plus, after seeing what I was able to do with this little side business with just a little guidance, she was hopeful that the advanced coaching would supercharge my efforts. Either way, she gave me the green light.

I joined Trey's coaching program and, sure enough, as soon as I had the road map of what I needed to do, everything changed. With my new understanding of how to properly do Facebook ads, combined with Trey's weekly coaching, my t-shirts started selling - like crazy. Turns out I wasn't a big dummy, I was just uneducated.

For one year, I remained in Trey's coaching program, sold shirts online and trained dogs. Although the shirts continued to sell, bringing me and my family some nice additional cash, my heart just wasn't in it. It was fun, but didn't leave me feeling fulfilled. It required a lot of my time and I wanted more out of it than just the money.

Training dogs really fills me up because I know I'm helping people. They are better off having spent time with me and that makes me happy. I think that being of service to others is the very best way to live and make a living. Even though I had cracked the online t-shirt selling code and was making money, I called it quits.

Once again, I had discovered that money did not equate to happiness.

In addition to learning how to create a successful e-commerce business and how to run Facebook ads, my experience with Trey taught me another valuable lesson that I would never forget. I re-learned the value of coaching. You see, Trey wasn't my first business coach, there was one before him (more on that a little later on in the book). I had just forgotten how important and valuable a coach could be. Alone, I struggled, wasting both time and money.

However, as soon as I found someone who was where I wanted to be and jumped under their wing, my success skyrocketed. Since my time with Trey, I have never been without a coach.

> "One of the greatest values of mentors is the ability to see ahead what others cannot see and to help them navigate a course to their destination."
>
> – John C. Maxwell

There's no way I'm going to do it the long, hard way again when I can find someone who can tell me exactly what I need to do and dramatically shorten my learning curve and help me reach my goals faster and easier. I think for most people who have never done any kind of coaching program, the expense seems high and there's no guarantee it will be worth it. Once you've done it though, and seen the results, it's a no brainer.

I highly recommend you find yourself a mentor and/or coach that is where you want to be and has done the things you want to do. The main reason you aren't where you want to be isn't because you can't do it, it's most likely because you just don't know how to do it.

In whatever area of your life you're struggling, find your mentor.

9

Going All In

I didn't need to set an alarm, my mind had been turning all night in anticipation of the morning. I peeked over at the nightstand clock as I carefully snuck out of bed, trying not to disturb my wife. It read 5:48AM. I smiled excitedly as I crept out of the bedroom and into the bathroom.

I have always been a morning person. My wife says that I pop out of bed like a piece of toast, angered by my ability to awaken instantly and in a good mood. My wife is not a morning person. If given the opportunity, she could sleep a whole day away and still be tired whenever she was forced to rise. Once awake, I feed her a steady flow of coffee for about an hour before I even think about conversing with her. One time I made the mistake of vacuuming the bedroom just after she woke up. The look she gave me is still tattooed on my brain and still resurfaces in my nightmares every so often.

I headed down to the kitchen and got a big glass of water, a bowl of cereal and moved into my small office. As I sat down in the comfy chair in front of my desk, I simultaneously turned on my computer - moving as quickly as I could. I knew that if all went well I would have about four straight hours until my wife got out of bed and I could get so much accomplished. The year was 2007 - the year before the twins entered our lives - forever changing weekend mornings for us. For now though, I had all Sunday mornings to myself and this was how I spent them all.

I typed in my login info as I shoveled a spoonful of cereal in my mouth. As the program loaded, I was downright giddy with excitement. After a few seconds (that seemed to take forever), I was in and staring at Udu, my troll priest. For the next four and a half hours, I was glued to my chair (with the exception of a few very quick bathroom breaks) and lost myself in the World Of Warcraft, the nerdy online role-playing game where you create characters and go on amazing adventures, fighting fearsome monsters and discovering all kinds of cool treasure.

I would love to tell you that playing video games for that length of time was a unique thing, but I would be lying big time. In fact, during this time in my life, I typically played for 2 - 4 hours a clip about every other day. Oh yeah, I was addicted.

Looking back now, I can't believe I wasted so much time staring at my computer, lost in some imaginary world. It's kind of sad, but I could happily do it again. That's addiction alright. I grew up playing Dungeons and Dragons, Atari video games and watched lots of fantasy movies. World Of Warcraft (aka WOW) combined all three of those - I didn't stand a chance.

For over a year, I invested countless hours in developing my characters, advancing their levels and amassing a pretty cool stash of armor, weapons and treasure. I had a bunch of friends that I had met in the game and we would meet up online and go on all kinds of fun adventures together. It was cool and I loved it.

Suddenly cutting it off forever was not an easy thing to do, but that's exactly what I did. It's not something I wanted to do, nor was it something I had to do. It's something I chose to do.

The day I made the decision to become a dog trainer was the day I left the World Of Warcraft forever. I understood that I was trying to do something I had never done before and knew nothing about. If I was going to be successful, I was going to have to learn as much as I could and devote myself to it. I had to go all in.

This was not my first complete career change. I had done it a few times before and was able to see success each time - all because I went all in. That means sacrificing some personal time and desires, and replacing them with education. I needed to immerse myself into dog training and use every available free minute to learn my new craft.

I wanted to get it rolling sooner rather than later and had this crazy notion of paying my bills on time too. That combined with my wife and I trying to start a family, made me pretty motivated to build this new business up as quickly as I could. So to help me do that, I used every second of free time I had for education.

In addition to going cold turkey on my video games, I also stopped listening to Howard Stern in the car - which I did on pretty much every drive. Both WOW and Howard were distractions in my life. They weren't moving me forward at all, just giving me a brief escape from the real world. This is okay to a certain degree, but not when you're trying to aggressively move your life forward.

I replaced all those wasted hours with reading books, taking courses and listening to podcasts. I switched all my down time from entertainment to education, which tends to lead to some really cool long-term results. So many people complain about not being where they want to be in life, saying they want success so badly and they just don't have the time to make their dreams happen. Yet, they have plenty of time to stare at the TV, watch sporting events and drink with their buddies on the weekends. Your schedule will always tell your truth. Where are you really spending your time?

Not playing World of Warcraft really sucked - I loved that damn game - but I saw the big picture. You need to make sacrifices in order to achieve things. Nothing comes easily or for free, you need to work for it. This is why there are so few ultra-successful people out there. Most people don't want to give stuff up but still want to do it all.

Everything comes at a price. You can learn how to do anything if you are willing to put in the time, learn what you need to do and make some sacrifices. It sounds simple and it kind of is - if you're motivated enough. The problem is that most people won't give up immediate pleasure for the possibility of something greater in the future. We tend to see only what's right in front of us and neglect looking ahead at what we could be building in the future by our present actions.

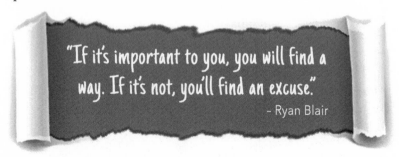

"If it's important to you, you will find a way. If it's not, you'll find an excuse."
- Ryan Blair

You need to be willing to commit to your goal and go all in. That means putting all of your energy and resources into reaching it.

Writing this book is a prime example. Just about everyone says they would like to write a book "some day." When asked what's stopping them, they have a long list of things that are more important or more pressing. Yet when you look at them, they still have plenty of time for their leisure activities. "Some day" never comes.

I'm typing this very chapter on a hot summer afternoon. My wife and kids went to the beach for the day, leaving me home with my Beagley buddy, Bowie. I would have loved to be at the beach right now, playing in the surf with my kids. However, I have my goal of finishing this book. I'm willing to sacrifice the day so that I can move this book forward and get it printing and in your hands as soon as possible.

I'm a pretty driven guy, so once I have my sights on something, it's not hard for me to go all in and give up much of my free time to help me achieve my goal. The problem that I have is that I get so consumed with making progress as fast as possible that I risk losing sight of the other important things in my life.

Going all in doesn't mean achieving your goals at the expense of your family and friends. Although I skipped the beach today, I will still make time for my wife and kids on the weekend. You shouldn't completely stop all the other non-goal activities of your life. Make time for the other important things in your life - just be honest about what is really important.

A few years ago, I was interviewed on a podcast for aspiring entrepreneurs. At the end of the interview, the host asked me a question he always asks at the end of every interview: "What's your favorite quote?"

I thought about it for a moment, pondering all the great quotes by Steve Jobs, Elon Musk, Richard Branson and the other business greats. They were all very inspiring and helpful. However, there was one quote that had helped me for decades. It was one that I'm pretty positive no other business interviewee has ever cited before. Years ago, I used to be a body builder (hard to believe, I know) and I used to carry a notebook to every work out where I recorded my progress in the gym so I could keep pushing myself. My goal at the time was to compete in a natural body building show. To keep me focused, I scribbled a quote on the front cover of that notebook:

"What you won't do, I will."

I looked at that every day and used it to keep me motivated and on track. Other people wouldn't go to the gym on Saturday, I would. Others wouldn't skip dessert, I would. Others wouldn't push through exercises that made them uncomfortable, I would. Everything they wouldn't do because they were not willing to pay the price, I would.

They say, "It's never crowded at the top." Why? Because very few want to do what it takes to get there. Sacrifices have to be made and hard work has to be done over and over again. It all comes down to what you really want and what you're willing to do to get it.

I looked at that quote every day for over a year, and it helped get me all the way to my first (and only) body building show, where

I took 3rd place . . . out of three people, so you could also say I got last place. That was totally cool with me though. My goal wasn't to win (although I would have gladly accepted that big trophy), it was just to be able to compete. I had so much fun during the show and was able to get into the best shape of my life, so I consider that a victory.

The funny thing about that quote is that it wasn't said by some giant business icon or famous motivational speaker, but by heavy metal rocker Marilyn Manson - and I took it completely out of context. I just heard the words randomly in a song and they stuck in my head. I still love it though and think it's a very powerful mantra for you to adopt when working toward any goal.

Now you don't have to (and shouldn't) sacrifice everything to reach your goals. I'm a firm believer in having fun along the way and using some of your downtime for whatever makes you smile. BUT, you have to prioritize diligently and decide what is really important to you. Then, once you commit to a goal, go all in.

I knew nothing about being a dog trainer when I made the choice to become one. I just decided that making a career in dog training was my priority. I moved all my down time from entertainment to education and gave it everything I had, which enabled me to move forward quickly and gain some great momentum.

If you do the same, you can achieve your goals, no matter what they are.

Do it. Go all in.

10

Ready, Fire, Aim

I have to admit, I was really nervous.

I got there early to give me plenty of time to set up and go over my notes. There were seven people signed up for class and they would be arriving with their dogs in about thirty minutes - whether I was ready or not.

I was standing in an empty dog daycare where I was going to be doing my obedience and puppy classes. About two months before, I had made the decision to teach my own classes, having really no idea how to do them. I knew that teaching group dog training classes was something I wanted to do, but wasn't really sure I could pull it off. I had zero experience teaching classes and only recently finished my initial dog trainer education. My only experience with group classes was taking my own dog to class and observing one. All in all, I really wasn't well-equipped to teach a class all by myself, yet very soon I would have to.

The last of the daycare dogs left a few minutes ago, as did the last daycare worker, leaving me alone in the building. Was this going to work? Would they all demand their money back? Would the dogs break free of their leashes and eat me? All the worst case scenarios went through my head as I looked over the syllabus I had jotted down for today's class.

The truth of the matter was I was in no way completely ready to teach my first obedience class, but that was okay. Even though I wasn't 100% sure I knew what I was doing, teaching the class was the right thing to do. It didn't matter if I wasn't totally confident and this was something I had never done before, it was something I had to do if I wanted my business to move forward.

If you wait until you're totally prepared, learned everything there is to know and wait for the timing to be perfect, you will never do anything. There's always more stuff you could do, more ways you could improve and additional ways you can get yourself more ready. It can go on and on, forever. And that's where many people get stuck - in preparation mode, too afraid they are not ready to ever pull the trigger. Time goes on and they never get to it.

It's much better to just go for it, make some mistakes, learn and adjust. That's the way to keep moving forward. You want to do some research and preparation, but just don't get trapped there, waiting for the "right moment". At some point you need to take a leap of faith and just go for it. Even if you don't hit your mark, you're closer to the goal than if you were still at the starting line.

If you fail, what happens?

Will you spontaneously combust, sending little bits of your body into the air at high speeds, covering everything around you in your guts?

Probably not.

So if exploding death is not an option, so what if you fail?

I've actually grown to like failure. Don't get me wrong, I'm pretty bummed out when things don't go my way and fail miserably (often in public). At the moment of failure, it sucks - but as long as I didn't spontaneously explode, it's going to be okay. Once you understand that failure is not final, but all part of the process toward success, you'll learn to appreciate it and it won't affect you as much.

Instead of failure being a final point of devastation, it's actually a stepping stone on your path to accomplishment. When Thomas Edison was trying to invent the lightbulb, he failed over and over again. When someone asked him about it he said, "I have not failed. I've just found 10,000 ways that won't work."

Every failure brings you closer to success.

When something I was working on didn't work out, I used to get really down and discouraged for days. If the goal was something really important that took lots of my time, effort and money, I might be in a funk for weeks.

Not anymore.

I've learned that as long as you learn from what happened, re-group and move on (even if it means abandoning the thing you were working toward), it is an asset that can help you in the future. Lessons learned from failure can prove much more valuable than if everything went perfectly.

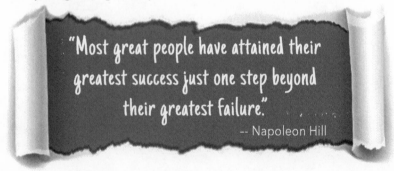

"Most great people have attained their greatest success just one step beyond their greatest failure."
-- Napoleon Hill

A couple of years ago I decided to create an online community dog training membership site. I was so excited about it and felt it was going to be huge. I created a number of different video courses, an interactive forum and did live coaching. I worked on the site for over a year and spent about $2,000 creating it. I thought people would go nuts for this and I was eager to be able to help so many people, not to mention I was hoping this would be a huge financial success.

I was wrong. It flopped and, within a few months, I had to close it down. I had wasted all that time and money and my failure was a very public one because I had promoted the site heavily and been talking about it for months. Everyone knew I had failed.

I think I was down in the dumps over that for about two days - no more.

By this time I had failed quite a few times throughout the years and had already learned that, although that's not how I wanted it to go, it was going to be okay. I immediately started writing in my journal all the reasons I felt it didn't work out and what I could learn from the experience. By understanding that failure is part of the process on the way to success, I was able to gain new insights that would have been unavailable to me if my mind wasn't open to it. I may revisit the project again in the future, with the lessons learned from the initial failure guiding me to do better the next time around. Even if I never bring it back, the experience from the first failure will help me in other things I do.

Don't let the fear of failure stop you. So many people allow their lives to be severely limited because they are afraid of things going south. I used to be one of them, but never again.

Now back to my first obedience class. The people started to arrive with their dogs and settled in a circle around the room. For the most part, the dogs were excited but surprisingly pretty well-behaved. Only one was a bit barky, while the others adjusted after only a few minutes. I introduced myself and we got started. I was a bit awkward trying to balance giving group directions while still trying to provide each person with some one-on-one attention. It definitely wasn't my best work, but I got through the class and everyone seemed to be satisfied.

Always remember, 99.9% of the time, if you fail, you're not going to spontaneously combust, so what's the worst that can happen? You can come back from just about anything - others have already proven that. I want you to think like Edison and see failure as a way to move closer to success.

Failure is only bad if you don't learn from it. Do your best to get ready, take action in spite of possible failure then move forward, whether it went as planned or not. This may sound easy, but it can actually be quite hard in reality until you've been through it a few times. Failure still always sucks no matter how often you've survived it. However, once you learn to accept it and not allow it to cripple you, you'll then be able to look for the golden nuggets of learning that are wrapped inside.

As you're setting your goals, working hard and occasionally failing, there's one thing you need to always keep in mind. The way to make things happen and rebound when things don't go well is by taking more action to move you away from where you are and toward where you want to go.

I have an uncle who is super religious. He is a very devout Catholic and has put all his faith in God. He also has big time financial problems, as well as difficulties finding long-term work. He's always struggling and can never seem to improve his situation - this has been going on for years and years and years. I'm not all that close to him and haven't seen him for years, but in the past when he would come over, he would go on and on about his troubles and explain how he keeps praying for things to change.

His problem is so clear to me . . . it's all that praying.

Now don't get me wrong, there is nothing wrong with being religious and having faith - that's not the problem (having some kind of spiritual focus is very beneficial.) The problem is my uncle only prays. He is waiting for God to "save him" but isn't doing his part. He takes no action at all, except to pray for help. He's just wishing upon a star, hoping things will get better and asking that his life be changed but without taking any kind of active part in his life. He's put his entire future in the hands of the cosmos. He's waiting for everything to be hand delivered to him instead of going out and finding it.

Prayer alone will not get you want you want. Wishing for something but doing nothing about it will not make things happen. Setting goals without taking action or moving yourself forward won't get them accomplished.

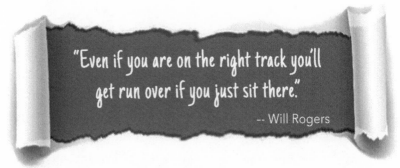

"Even if you are on the right track you'll get run over if you just sit there."

-- Will Rogers

My uncle doesn't understand that everything he needs is available to him, all he has to do is go get it. Taking action is the key. Most of the time things are not going to just land in your lap. It's not like ordering room service. You can't just sit in your room waiting for the world to deliver your dreams to you. Prayer, wishing and goal setting are all valuable, but they are only the starting point. It's like building this amazing sports car that's capable of going zero to sixty in seconds flat. It looks awesome, but it's not moving at all. To get it to move, you need to put gas in the tank and physically drive it. You are the gasoline and spark that will make your life move forward. If you don't fuel up and put your foot on the accelerator, you're going nowhere.

When I first started reading a lot of personal development books, many of them recommended creating vision boards. I cut out pictures of all the things I wanted in my life: new car, fancy house, vacations, business location, etc. Then every day, I stared at the images and focused on what I wanted. You know what happened? Nothing.

Vision boards alone weren't going to do anything if I didn't take the actions that would make acquiring the things on my board possible. It's not that vision boards are not great tools, just like prayer, wishes and goals, but that alone will not do much. You can't just wait for things to move to you, you need to move toward the things you want. You are a very important and active component in this process.

Action, even the wrong action, will get you closer to your goals because you will learn from your failures and adjust your next actions. Think about it; an object at rest stays at rest. The more stuff you do, the more stuff will happen to you. Keep taking action until you discover the right steps that will help you accomplish all your goals, make your wildest dreams come true and answer all your own prayers.

Success starts with a wish, is crystallized into a goal, is then charged up by prayer and delivered with constant and repeated action.

11

Emptying Your Cup

It was a simple question and she was patiently waiting for my response. However, I really wasn't sure how to answer her. Although it seemed like something that I should be able to respond to very easily, the truth is I never really thought about it until she asked it.

Since this conversation took place many years ago, I've been asked this question countless times and am now ready for it and have a proper answer waiting. Back when it was first asked to me by this woman, I was a relatively new (I had only been working with dogs for less than a year) and was still trying to figure out where I fit in within the dog trainer landscape.

Seeing my glazed over look and lack of response must have made her thought I didn't hear her question, because she repeated it: "So, what kind of trainer are you?"

Feeling bad that she had to repeat the question again, I opened my mouth but stopped myself before any words could come out. I wanted to answer her, but didn't quite know how to articulate it. I'm sure she felt it was a straight forward question and not one that should stump me, so I could only assume she thought I had the mental capacity of a loaf of bread.

Why was this so damn hard for me to answer??

I didn't really understand it back then, but now I know it's a complicated question for me because I'm very unlike many of my dog trainer colleagues. What you may not know (I sure didn't when I first got into the industry) is that the dog training world is very polarized between different training methodologies. There are positive dog trainers, dog whisperers, clicker trainers, "balanced" trainers, and a whole bunch more. Each philosophy has different beliefs about dogs and rules of how you should work with them. Although there is a good degree of overlap between many of the factions, they typically don't mix with each other. In fact, they often violently disagree and only come together to yell and argue about which is the better way to train dogs.

I found this very surprising and tremendously disappointing. I assumed that since we're all in the same industry, trying to accomplish the same goals, that we would all be on the same team. I was expecting that we would be supporting each other and working together to further our businesses and the industry as a whole. I couldn't have been more wrong.

I was shocked to find that many of them hated each other and drew very sizable lines in the sand, where you were either with them or against them. They wanted you to take a side and, if you wouldn't, they assumed you were with "the enemy". Not everyone was like this and I do think it's getting better over time, but back in the beginning of my career as a dog trainer, it could get pretty brutal.

My problem was that I didn't really fit into any category completely and refused to takes sides, so I was sort of an outcast.

Not choosing a single training camp was kind of unheard of (although now, it's becoming more common) and the other trainers didn't know what to make of me.

So my answer to, "what kind of trainer are you?" typically goes like this. I'm the mutt of the dog training world. There is no one person or training methodology that I agree with 100%. I take bits and pieces from many different dog training philosophies and mash them together to create my own unique style. I'm an open minded guy in general and consider myself an open minded trainer. I believe this makes my toolbox rather large, enabling me to help a wide variety of people, dogs and situations.

I've come to this conclusion after years of experimentation and trial and error. The two main dog training empires are Positive Dog Training, led by Ian Dunbar and Victoria Stilwell, and Dog Whispering, headed by Cesar Millan. After trying out what both sides teach, I see that both have their merits and shortcomings. I just take my favorite principals - the ones that I've tested out and have worked well - and leave what I don't care for.

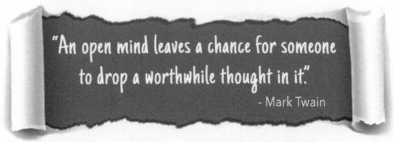

"An open mind leaves a chance for someone to drop a worthwhile thought in it."
- Mark Twain

My journey started out by reading Cesar Millan's first book, which really helped me with my Pit Bull, Hayley. He was my introduction into the world of dog behavior training. I had assumed from my limited exposure to dog training that it was all just teaching obedience to get compliance. Cesar helped me understand that, to change our dog's behavior, we needed to change ours. This was an amazing concept to me and had pretty immediate effects on my relationship with my dog.

Once I decided to make dog training my career, I started to dive deeper into the dog whispering world. I was encouraged by my personal success and wanted to help others achieve the same results with their dogs. That's where the trouble started.

When I started to work with dogs with more challenging issues like fear, anxiety and aggression, the dog whispering way started to unravel. The more I pushed these types of dogs, the worse things got. Not only was it not working, but I felt, in many cases, I was setting the dogs up to fail - and putting myself and my clients in harm's way (in the form of pointy teeth).

I knew something wasn't right and there must be something I was missing. I knew in my gut that these dogs could be helped - I just didn't know how to do it. That led me to start doing some more research and exploring some other ways to work with dogs. During my hours of online searches on how to train dogs, one name kept coming up, time and time again, Ian Dunbar.

Ian is one of the most respected dog behavior and training experts on the planet. He used to be a veterinarian, had one of the first dog training television shows and researched dogs in scientific settings for years. It quickly became clear that he knew his stuff and is someone I should be paying attention to, so I dove head first into everything that Ian put out. Ian is the founder of the positive dog movement and created the Association of Professional Dog Trainers (APDT), the national organization for positive dog trainers, and has dedicated the last decade or two to educating dog trainers on "science based dog training".

I soaked all of Ian's content in and immediately started using it with my clients. The results were impressive. I was now able to help dogs in ways I couldn't before, my clients were happy and I felt better about the tools I had. Positive dog training worked!

After some time went on and my experiments in dog training continued, I realized that I liked chunks of what both Cesar and Ian taught, but not everything. Since I have studied both training styles, I can mix and match what I feel is best suited for the individual dog and person in front of me at the time. So, I'm not a dog whisperer or a positive dog trainer, or any other one kind of dog trainer. Currently, I'm heavily weighted toward positive dog training, just because that's the one that works the best for me. However, I still utilize many "dog whisperer" ideas.

I think the key takeaway here is to always have an open mind and always be open to learning new ideas - even if they are different than what you currently believe. This is where I see so many dog trainers fall short. They are so consumed with their current beliefs that they completely block out anything that doesn't go along with that. If you think you know it all, you will never learn anything new ever again.

I love this quote by Nyogen Senzaki, who was a Rinzai Zen monk and one of the 20th century's leading proponents of Zen Buddhism in the United States.

> "Like this cup, you are full of your own opinions and speculations. How can I show you wisdom unless you first empty your cup?"

So many people are walking around with their cups filled up to the brim and they're unable to take in anything more. Drink up what you learn but keep that cup empty so you can fill it again. Nobody knows it all and we are all works in progress.

If you can remove your attachment to your beliefs and be open to hearing new ideas (it doesn't mean you have to agree with or use them), you will be increasing your skills and knowledge every single day. Every once in a while, I lose track of things and I start to get a bit full of myself, thinking that I'm so smart when it comes to dog behavior and training. Then some dog will come along and figuratively smack me across the face, helping me realize that I still have so much to learn.

Many years ago I attended a seminar by dog trainer and author, Sarah Wilson. To be honest, I can't remember what the topic of her talk was or anything specific about her presentations - except for her very first sentence. After all this time, I still remember her first words that day because I thought it was such a great attitude to have. Sarah stepped in front of the audience, introduced herself and said, "The following is what I currently believe but that may change by the next time you see me." I love that. She's showing us she has an open mind and that, even though she's there as the expert, she's still learning along the way.

My dad and my brother are both medical doctors, so it would seem that medicine is in my genetics (although it's never something I considered - it's just not for me). One thing I love about doctors is the way they phrase their businesses - they have a medical "practice". With that simple phrase, they are emphasizing that they will never know it all, will always be learning new things and forever have an open mind. Even though many doctors out there seem to have forgotten this, I think it's something that every industry needs to adopt.

Whatever you do, make it a practice. Always keep your mind open to learning new things - even from unlikely sources. This actually happens to me all the time in The FernDog Trainer Academy. As I'm working with students, teaching them what I know about dog training, behavior and how to run a successful business, they are constantly helping me learn new things. My students teach me just as much as I teach them, and I'm learning so much because I'm open to it.

Empty your cup, be open minded and continually evolve who you are. That's the only way to keep improving and moving forward in business and in life.

12

Part Time Rocket Fuel

You may not know this about me, but I'm an expert on poop. It's not something I tell most people or am particularly proud of, but it's a fact. It wasn't an intentional endeavor but more of an unexpected side effect. My poop skills are limited, though. I'm not proficient in all kinds of poop, just dog poop.

I didn't go out to learn and study poop (what kind of a guy do you think I am?) or go out of my way to put myself in the path of poop. It was just all around me and it was my job to grab it as quickly as I could, ideally before another dog ran over and tried to eat it (and no, I don't know for certain why some dogs think poop is a delicacy).

When I decided to become a dog trainer, I wanted to study with the top experts in the field of dog behavior. In my opinion, the number one authority on dogs is ... wait for it ... dogs. I needed to go to the source and spend as much time as I could with my furry mentors, soaking up everything they had to teach me.

That's what led me into the lobby of Rover Ranch and Spa in Fairfield, New Jersey. I walked in and asked for a job working with the daily daycare packs. Lucky for me, they needed some extra help and I was able to start immediately. I worked part time supervising the dogs in the play groups, making sure everyone behaved and had a good time. In addition to supervising them, I also had the glamorous task of pack beautification - aka elimination evangelist, aka facility de-stinkifier, aka picking up poop - lots of it.

The job didn't pay much, but was a critical step to making the transition into my new career as a dog trainer. Remember, I was starting from zero, had no idea what I was doing or how to get this new career off the ground. I also desperately needed to find a way to pay some bills before my wife decided that marrying for money instead of love was a better idea.

I knew I was going to need some time to learn my new craft and that building my business would happen slowly over time. If I got a part time job that brought in a little money, it would take some of the financial pressure off and allow me the time I needed to get my education and get my new business off the ground.

There was a number of other part time jobs I could have taken that would have paid more money and been less stinky. My many past careers left me with a variety of skills that I could utilize for a side job. However, I was thinking of the big picture.

By taking a job in a dog daycare, I would not only be bringing in some much needed money, but would also be helping my dog training career. I would get to hang out with dogs all day, accruing valuable dog time, which helped me better understand dog behavior and how to work with them. Secondly, I was getting in front of my ideal clients every day, enabling them to get to know me so they might be comfortable hiring me to help them with their dogs someday. And finally, it allowed me to build a relationship with the daycare and its owner, which would serve me for years. Although my paycheck was rather modest and a good portion of my day was spent picking up poop, it was an investment in my future.

Once you decide on a new career path, you should take advantage of everything available that will help move you forward long-term - always think big picture! If I just took the job that paid the most so I could make more money (which I seriously considered) without the vision of what would move me forward the most, I would have seriously handicapped my success.

Look at the industry you're going into and identify some other parallel businesses that, although not exactly what you want to do, have your ideal customer base and can provide you with some additional knowledge. The first few years I was a dog trainer, I had jobs at two different dog daycares as well as a pet store. All of those paid just over minimum wage, but the skills I learned there have helped grow my dog training career and were actually a driving force to my success.

At the holistic pet shop where I worked, I cleaned up bird cages (expanding my poop knowledge - yippee), stocked shelves and worked the register (something I never could quite figure out). It also put me in close proximity to the store's owner, who happened to be a canine nutrition guru and a dog trainer. He was my very first mentor and taught me canine wellness, which is an asset that has helped so many of my clients over the years.

Building a business also takes time. Unless you have a large nest egg of savings or have wealthy parents who don't mind funding you as you start your new career, you're going to need some cash. If you can't pay your bills, you won't have the time needed to get your initial education and create the foundation of your new business. The lack of predictable money coming in will lead to boatloads of stress and may force you to abandon your dream before it's even had a realistic chance of success.

Just having a little money coming in will help give you the time needed to get your foundation built and your new business moving along. Remember, you won't be working these jobs forever, it's just until you get the ball rolling. You're just using this part time job(s) as a leverage point to stabilize your current income and boost your new business along.

Diving into a brand new career is totally doable. However, you will need a runway to build momentum and set yourself up for long-term success. Taking a part time job within the industry you're getting into, even if it's not ideally what you want to do, can provide positive shock waves that your business will ride for years to come.

13

No More Empty Seats

I pulled my car into a parking spot right in front of the school. It was 10:45AM on a Tuesday, so there were plenty of open spaces, since the rest of the world was busy at work. Not me though, not right now. I had more important things to do - much more important.

I walked to the front of the school, pressed the button at the main doors and was soon buzzed inside. I joined a few other parents who were already waiting right outside the main office doors. After a few minutes, we were led upstairs and into the music room, where about twenty chairs were set up in messy rows behind an upright piano.

I took a seat somewhere in the middle close to the front. The chairs were built for grade school kids and made my six foot, one inch frame feel a bit awkward. I exchanged a humorous smile with one of the moms next to me as we both tried to get comfortable in the small chairs. Once everyone was seated, the music teacher, Mrs. Foster, explained that she had invited us to see what our kids were working on and get a peek into how the music classes were run.

Mrs. Foster was new to the school (this was her first year), and this informal event was just a way for the parents to get to know her. As far as I know, no other teacher had ever done anything like this and I thought it was a nice way for us to get a rare window into what our children really did while they were in school.

As I tried to find some way to get comfortable in my mini chair, the kids filed in and sat on the floor between the piano and the parents. When my daughter Sabrina walked in, she immediately scanned the room, looking for me (she knew I was coming). Once her eyes met mine, her face erupted into an ear to ear smile and she threw me a little wave. Seeing her so happy to see me there really warmed my heart.

She was eight years old and I had a feeling that it wouldn't be long before her and her twin sister wanted little to do with me, once their adolescent agendas kicked in. My girls were growing up so fast and I knew that I would soon go from "cool dad" to "annoying father." For now I was treasuring each and every moment I had with them and was so grateful to be able to come to all the events in their lives.

Mrs. Foster settled the kids down and began their music lesson. As I watched Sabrina sing and interact with her friends and the teacher, I found myself smiling widely as well. I glanced around at the other parents and noticed quite a few empty chairs among us. There were 24 kids in class but only a handful of parents present.

This was a common theme at school events since so many parents are unable to get the time off of work to see their kid's events during the day. Knowing how happy Sabrina was to see me at this, and all her activities, made me sad for the other parents who have to continually miss out on moments like this one. Childhood is such an amazing and important time for both kids and parents.

Although raising young kids is not easy (I'm not proud of the yelling I did this morning), it's also incredibly fun. As I watch my girls growing up, I'm happy to see the young ladies they are turning into, but also a bit sad, knowing they will soon be leaving these carefree, innocent years of childhood behind.

I watched as Sabrina tried to hit a high note and started giggling with one of her friends at the sound that came out of her mouth. It is times like these I'm so happy to be a dog trainer. While so many parents are confined to their jobs, unable to be at all the events of their kids' lives, I haven't missed a single one yet. My daughters know when they look out into the audience, they'll always see me there.

As a dog trainer working for myself, I get to control my schedule and decide what I want to do and when. I'm able to prioritize my family over my job and make sure I'm there when my kids need or want me. To me, that's everything. It's so much fun getting to work with dogs all day and very rewarding to know that I'm helping the people that I work with. However, having complete control over my time is probably my favorite thing about being a dog trainer.

Traditional 9 to 5 jobs have it all wrong. If you're like most people and work for someone else, you get your work schedule and then have to squeeze your personal life around that. I do the opposite. I figure out all the things I WANT to do and then schedule my work around it. This allows me to live life on my terms and never miss out on anything important.

My mom tells me daily how much she misses the time when my brother and I were young kids. As my kids grow up, I too miss the time gone by, but I don't have any regrets about it because I know I was there for all of it and got the most out of that precious time.

Being an entrepreneur has enabled me to create a life of my choosing. My days are not dictated by someone else and I don't have to ask anyone for permission to take time off or justify why I'm at a 3rd grade music class in the middle of the day on a Tuesday. I choose it all.

Time is the most valuable resource we have. You can always make more money but you can never make more time. Once this moment right now is gone, you can never get it back. I'll never be able to go back to when my kids were in 3rd grade. I won't get another chance to experience those school plays, gymnastic practices or roller skating parties ever again. Lucky for me, I was there for all those, and more.

When elderly people toward the end of their life are asked what they regret most, nobody ever says they wished they worked more. Instead, they say they wish they'd spent more time with their family and friends. They wished they made more memories early on and used their time on the things that are really important in life.

"The bad news is time flies. The good news is that you're the pilot."

- Michael Altshuler

Being an entrepreneur allows me the flexibility to do what I want, but it does come at a price. When I'm at my daughter's music class, I'm not working, so I'm not making any money. And, although money isn't the most important thing in life, it's still necessary. By taking so much time off to be there to drop my kids off at school, take them to practices and help them with their homework every afternoon (well, sort of - damn you new math!), I have to sacrifice some income. To me, it's well worth it because my family is the most important thing in my life.

The cool thing about being a dog trainer is that most of the work happens in the evening and weekends, so it's perfect if you have young kids. I will occasionally do some appointments during the weekdays, but most of it comes when the 9 to 5'ers are off from work.

No matter when the work comes though, I decide when I want to do it and, if something for my kids comes up unexpectedly (which happens surprisingly more than you would think), I'm there without a problem. For me, the ability to control my time - the most important resource in the world - is critical to me being happy. It allows me to control how I spend my limited time here on Earth, enabling me to squeeze the juice out of life on a daily basis.

This wasn't always true for me though. There was a time early on in my dog training career where I lost track of my priorities and got caught up in the quest for money and business success. It was back in my third or fourth year as a dog trainer. I had worked hard and was able to build my business into a success, all while still being a stay-at-home-dad for my girls. Raising one child isn't easy, but bringing up twins is utterly exhausting (anyone with triplets is my ultimate superhero). Yet, I was somehow doing it, while also creating a solid dog training business.

Then I saw my first business coach and he asked me a simple question that changed my life.

By now you know I like to create some build-up with these questions that were asked of me. So before I tell you what this life altering question was, I want to have a quick chat about coaching (business or otherwise). We talked about why having a mentor is useful earlier with my experience with Trey Lewellen, my second business coach. About a year before that, I had my very first experience with a coach.

It took me a while to pull the trigger on paying for professional coaching because I, like many others, was uncertain of their value. The good ones tend to cost a lot and often you really don't get anything immediately tangible in return (the results take some time to see), which makes it hard to justify the expense. All coaching really is is advice. You're paying for someone else's advice. Is that really worth the money? Good coaches ain't cheap either - they require a sizable investment.

Ahhhh, there's that magic word again - "investment". Coaching, like all education, is not a gamble, it's an investment in yourself. If you choose the right coach *and* do the work, you will be making an invaluable investment into your success. People are always hesitant about hiring their first coach, but easily splurge for the second and third because, once you see the power of getting expert coaching, you'll find it a necessity.

A coach is someone who's done what you want to do, has been there, done that, and made the mistakes so you don't have to. You get to leverage their experience to greatly shorten your learning curve. A good coach can save you eons of time and boat loads of wasted money. Sure you could stumble around on your own and maybe figure things out eventually, but it might come at a pretty high cost (like your time and sanity). Sometimes without the right guidance, success is an impossibility.

It's like finding someone with a map that shows you exactly where to go and what to avoid, to get where you want to go. Why would you just walk around blindly when there's a guy willing to sell you the map so you can speed right there?

Everyone understands the value of coaching in sports. Good players and teams never seem to reach their potential until they find the right coach to bring out the best in them and to help them make the right choices to achieve success. It's really the same thing in any area of life, and if you look at successful people in any field - those at the top of their game - they all have coaches every step of the way.

Okay, back to my first coach and his question that changed my life. I had been following a number of people online, reading their books, listening to their podcasts and watching their videos. I was soaking in as much as I could from my virtual mentors and was seeing some results because of their teachings.

Chris Ducker was (and still is) one of my favorites. He's an expert in personal branding and has created a number of successful businesses for himself and produces a lot of content teaching how he did it. I was at a place where I knew I needed more personal help to move me forward, but wasn't sure how to get it. Then I heard that Chris was coming to New York and was doing a single day of coaching with a very small group (only 10 people).

I was very excited about this because Chris lives in the Philippines and doesn't make it over to the U.S. all that much. I was doubly excited when I heard the price, only $250 for the day - a steal (this was the first time Chris had done this and the price doubled the next year he did it). Even though the cost was so low, I was still a little hesitant. Would it really be worth my money and taking the whole day to jump the moat (aka the Hudson River) and go into New York City?

After a quick email exchange with Chris, I decided to give it a try and secured the very last spot. The way the day worked was, we met in a conference room in a building right in the Times Square area of the city and each person would be given about 30 minutes to go over what they wanted help with and get feedback from the group and guidance from my man, Ducker.

Everyone was in a different line of business and it was interesting hearing what they were working on and how they were overcoming their obstacles and moving toward their goals. Everyone in the group would offer tips and Chris would then give his advice on the best course of action for each individual. I was the very last person to go and had a hard time being patient, waiting for my turn to finally come.

When it did, I quickly described my business and described what my goals were, as well as the challenges I was facing. I explained how I was working and detailed what I thought my next steps might be. When I was done spewing it all out, I took a deep breath and waited for Chris to give me an action plan.

Chris looked at me quietly for a long moment, then asked me a simple, yet powerful question (yes, the one that would change my life). He asked me, "What's the most important thing in your life?"

I was confused. I was ready for a plan - I wanted to know what I should do. I didn't want questions, I wanted answers.

He repeated his question, "What's the most important thing in your life?"

Not quite understanding why he was asking this, but knowing the answer, I replied, "My family."

"No it's not," Chris shot back.

I was stunned. What the hell was Ducker trying to do? Of course my family is the most important thing in my life. How dare he even suggest otherwise and why was he wasting my limited time with this nonsense? He should be bestowing me with some amazing business insights, not asking stupid personal questions.

Seeing my confusion, he continued, "I'm sorry, Fern, but your schedule says you're lying."

Chris then pointed out something that I had somehow missed. I was working seven days a week, hustling my butt off to make my business a success. If my family was indeed the most important thing in my life, I would be spending more time with them. Your schedule always tells your truth. Where you spend your time shows your true priorities and I had mine all mixed up.

Sitting there in that conference room, everything become clear in an instant. I saw how I was working like crazy and not spending time with the people I cared about the most. My business success would come at the cost of missing some of the most treasured time with my wife and kids. How could I have missed this? How could I have not seen what I was sacrificing?

> "It's very important to prioritize. I know, for me, my family comes first. That makes every decision very easy."
> – Jada Pinkett Smith

I now know that I'm not alone. Many people work long hours, day in and day out, and end up missing what's really important in life. Lucky for me, with the help of Chris Ducker, I realized what I was doing before it was too late.

You can't get so caught up in your work that you lose sight of what matters most. Always keep your priorities in mind and constantly check to make sure you're living a life that supports them. That simple question Chris asked me was one of the most powerful in my life and I'll forever be grateful for him making me aware of it before too much time passed.

Now I knew I had messed up, but how was I going to fix things? I still wanted to grow my business and had bills to pay, but needed to make more time for my family. It seemed like a no-win situation. Once again, Chris had just what I needed. He told me to simply double my dog training rates, lose half of my clients but make exactly the same amount of money. That would enable me to work less, be with my family more and make exactly the same amount of money. It was so simple, yet brilliant.

Raising your prices even a little - let alone doubling them - is a scary thing for businesses. You never know how your customers will respond. I assumed they would be pissed off and go elsewhere for dog training. Upping my prices might shoot me right out of business.

In the end, I chickened out and just raised my prices by about 50%. The cool thing is that I really didn't lose any clients and was able to take Sundays off to spend with my family (a tradition I keep to this day). Since then, I've even shortened my work week further so I can spend even more time with my kids (my true priority), and it's been amazing.

My time with Chris Ducker opened my eyes to the amazing power of having a coach to help you and, since then, I make sure I always have a mentor (or two) in my life to supercharge my progress and help me avoid any pitfalls. It's always been worth every penny and has helped me decrease my stress, increase my success and help me lead a much happier life.

Once you know what you want, find someone with the map, allow them to accelerate your process, but always keep your priorities in mind.

14

I'm Not A Dog Person

I was a combination of nervous and excited as I pulled into the campus and looked for a parking spot. This was kind of a big deal to me and I really wanted to do a good job.

I was invited to speak at Rutgers University in New Brunswick, New Jersey, to give a talk for the Animal Science Department on having a career as a dog trainer. I would be telling the students about what it's like being a dog trainer so that they could determine if it might be something they would want to pursue. Although I'm pretty comfortable speaking in public, I had never spoken to this many people at once. The head of the department had seen one of my videos online and reached out to see if I would come speak to about 100 junior and senior students. Speaking at a University was actually on my bucket list, so I jumped at the chance.

This one talk actually became the catalyst for me pursuing a real speaking career. I enjoyed sharing my knowledge and interacting with the audience so much that I decided to make it a large chunk of my time going forward. Once I returned home from this first talk, I immediately started looking for more opportunities to speak and was fortunate to get booked at a number of conferences during the next year. Now speaking is one of my favorite things to do and one of my main business focuses.

For that first talk over at Rutgers, I was up in the front of a long, rectangular room with rows of tables on either side of the room, separated by a center aisle. Once everyone was settled in their seats, I spoke for about 45 minutes and then opened up the floor to questions. I was pleasantly surprised to find that most of the students were not only awake by the end of my talk, but also fairly engaged and all of their questions were thoughtful and very relevant.

When the class period ended, I thanked everyone for their time and began packing up my laptop. As the kids filed out of the room, a few approached me to ask an additional question or two. A young lady with long, dark hair and shy eyes thanked me, telling me that she really enjoyed my talk. She went on to say that she's been considering a career as a dog trainer and then said something that made me think she would never be able to achieve success in the field. It's actually something I've heard a number of dog trainers tell me and it makes me wince every time.

She said that she wants to be a dog trainer because she's more of a "dog person" than a "people person." I've also heard this said as, "I like dogs more than people."

The reason that statements and attitudes like this are so dangerous is that, as a dog trainer, your clients are not the dogs, they are the people. The dogs are not the ones paying you - the people are. Also, you need to be able to work with the people so that they can take what you teach and put it into practice on a daily basis. Dog training is actually more about the people than it is about the dogs.

My clients are often surprised to find that most of my time is spent speaking with them and not working with their dog. My job is not really to train their dog. My job is to train them to train their dog because I only have a small window of time with their pooch. They need to be the ones implementing my advice and doing all the hands-on stuff. The best use of my time is making sure I can accurately communicate what needs to be done to the people involved so they can do the homework. I always tell my clients that, if I'm doing my job appropriately, they should need me as little as possible.

If you're not a people person, you will fail as a dog trainer. In fact, having good people skills will help you in just about every single job or situation you'll ever find yourself in. No matter what you do for a living, you will have to interact with people, and your ability to communicate with others will have an effect on your success. That's why I believe cultivating your people skills is so important.

Much of my success as a dog trainer is my ability to work with people effectively. It's a skill that I've worked at over the years and completed a fair share of education on. Most dog trainers love learning all the dog stuff, but the business stuff and people skills get brushed aside and put off. However, without those skills, you'll never be successful long-term or, at the very least, will have a much harder time of it.

Luckily for me, one of my past careers really helped me hone my ability to understand and communicate with the people I'm working with. During my time as a personal trainer, I worked with people one-on-one who wanted to get in shape and increase their overall wellness. Physical fitness, at the time, was very important to me and I really loved helping people get healthier and feel better about themselves.

When I first become a personal trainer, I made a big mistake and found myself struggling to get clients. Around that time, I was very into weight training (this is when I competed in that natural body building show), so my personal focus was on building muscle. So when I started to work with other people, I just trained them like I trained myself. It seemed logical to me, but as a business strategy, it was tragically flawed.

Training everyone like I trained myself would be great if my clients were all young, aspiring body builders. They were not. The people I trained were average people typically between the ages 40 and 60. Not surprisingly, they really didn't care about having large pecs or being able to squat 400 lbs. I quickly learned that I couldn't train a soccer mom like I would train myself. My clients had different needs, limitations and wanted very different things. Assuming they would be happy with what I felt was important was a huge mistake, and my lack of success in those early days proved it.

Then one day I realized my blunder and changed my approach. I got out of my own head and tried to put myself in theirs. I asked lots of questions and actually listened to them. Listening is not a skill I was really good at. When someone was talking to me on a topic I was knowledgeable in and that I enjoyed, I would be thinking about what I was going to say as soon as they shut up (or, even worse, I would get impatient and cut them off mid-sentence.) Basically, I wasn't listening at all.

Once I started to forget myself and really try to understand what their story was, what their situation was like and what their goals and dreams were, I was able to create an exercise program that was exactly what they were looking for. Once I did that, everything changed. My clients started seeing the results they were looking for, enjoyed the workouts and started to refer their friends to me.

Although I'm far from perfect (just ask my wife), I now do my best to be an active listener, focusing on their words and giving the other person all my attention. Listening is such an undervalued and underutilized skill that really makes all the difference in building strong relationships with people.

In her book, "The Zen of Listening," Rebecca Shafir recommends "putting yourself in someone else's movie". When you are watching a movie you get lost in the characters, immersing yourself in what's happening and feeling the emotions of each moment. You can do the same thing with anyone you're speaking with. Try to put yourself in their story. Listen to what they are saying and put yourself into the situations and try to feel what they are experiencing. Having empathy for the person opposite you is the single most important aspect of any relationship you're trying to build. If you do your best to understand where the other person is coming from, you can create a favorable encounter.

Later on, as I started my dog training career, I was able to draw on my experience in working with people, listening to them and then creating a plan that worked for their individual needs. This enabled me to create a sizable client base of people whom I was able to serve properly, as well as who would go out of their way to refer me. I call them *The FernDog Army*. They are my happy customers who are out in the world doing all my marketing and promotion for me.

> "You learn when you listen. You earn when you listen - not just money but respect."
> - Harvey Mackay

Without effective people skills you will fail in dog training and struggle in just about everything. Everything you do will include interaction with others. If you learn to relate and communicate with them well, your life will improve and you will become more successful in the things that you do.

Another big mistake I see many dog trainers make is judging their clients. The person will be using training methods or tools that they don't agree with and they immediately judge them as bad people. They talk down to them and make them feel badly for what they are doing with their dog. That's not a great way to build rapport or get people to like you.

I tell my students to always remember that people are not trying to do the wrong thing - they are just doing the best they can with the information they have in front of them. They don't think they are doing anything wrong. If anything, they are just misinformed, so give them a break. People don't need your judgment, they just need some open mindedness and a fresh outlook.

It also doesn't matter what I would do in a particular situation, it's about what the client is able and willing to do. If you try to get someone to do something they are unable to do because of their unique circumstance or give them an option they don't care for or want, they will never be successful and neither will you. Instead, understand what they are capable of and listen to what they want, and then create a plan that will work for them.

I've actually gotten a number of clients just because their first trainer didn't have good people skills. It's worth practicing and improving over time. No matter what you want to do, become a people person and work on your interpersonal techniques.

15

Don't You Dare Call Me The "A" Word

"**A**re you crazy? Do you know what the average dog trainer makes?" asked one of my friends when I told him about my new career choice. I guess this might be a legitimate question to some people if they have a certain mindset, but it was totally irrelevant to me.

Dogs were my passion and working with them professionally was something I really believed would make me happy. I had learned earlier in life that money doesn't equate to happiness and, although I wasn't getting into dog training for the money, a guy's gotta eat, right?

If you do a Google search for "dog trainer salary" this comes up:

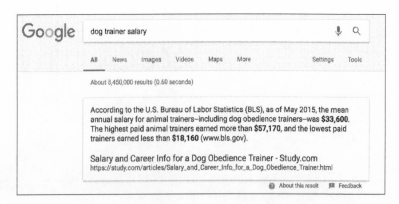

If I just went by that, then I guess my buddy would be right. I'll never support a family on an average dog trainer salary of $33,600 in Northern New Jersey. To me, there's some problems with this though. Forget the fact that not everything you read on the internet is true, my big problem is that one word: average.

Looking online, I saw people like Cesar Millan and Victoria Stilwell doing pretty well with book deals and television shows. Then I found a whole lot of other dog trainers that weren't celebrities but had really nice businesses going for themselves. I then realized that dog training is just like every other industry – there were people struggling to make a buck, others who were killing it and whole bunch in the middle somewhere.

Personally, I never go into anything with hopes of achieving the average results. Think about it, do you go into a relationship with someone hoping to have an average time? Do you go out to a restaurant for an average meal? Do you play a basketball game trying to be as average as you can?

No, no and no. So why on Earth would you set your sights on average when looking into a new career?

I couldn't care less what the "average" dog trainer made. All I wanted to know was what the top people were making. What did the upper levels of success look like? That's what I would be shooting for. That's what I was planning on.

The people who told me I couldn't make a lot of money as a dog trainer were riding the average train. They were playing the victim and blaming external forces for their lack of income. I had no plans of being an average dog trainer. No way. If other people were seeing lots of success and making good money doing it, then so could I.

Don't ever underestimate the human mind. Whatever you focus on, you will likely find. If you set your sights on average, don't be surprised if you end up there. Conversely, if you put all your energy and effort in being the best and never settle for average, there's not much you can't accomplish. The worst thing you can call me is average. That would be the harshest insult you could bestow upon me and a sure fire way to hurt my feelings.

I would never, ever, ever go into something hoping to be average. Average is ordinary. Don't strive to be ordinary - BE EXTRAORDINARY. You can't see me right now, but know that as I type this, I'm yelling this at you and throwing my hands in the air because that's how fired up this gets me. I don't want you to settle for an average anything - I will not hear of it. You deserve so much more than average.

And, do you want to know the really cool thing? Getting better than average isn't some unknown mystery. It's reachable to anyone who has the guts to go after it. You just have to really want to be extraordinary, then learn how to do it and work hard to get there. If you want it bad enough, it's readily available.

The biggest factor in getting off the average train is your attitude. Do you think of yourself as average? If you do, you'll be average for life. We already discussed the power of your thinking and how impactful it is on what happens to you, so you know that you need to be aware of your thought patterns. If you have a habit of talking yourself down and being negative, you'll usually default there. If that's the case, as it was with me, you'll need to be very conscious of your thinking and work on your self-worth.

We are always hardest on ourselves and it's always unwarranted criticism. The simple fact is that you don't understand how truly amazing you are and are undervaluing your gifts, which is severely limiting your success. Once you get out of your own way and realize there's nothing you can't do, you'll realize your potential and explode out of average and into extraordinary.

My wife, Michele, is a coach for a program called Girls on the Run, which is a like a combination running club and personal development course for young girls (ages 7-12ish). They meet weekly and learn how to do distance running, culminating in everyone running an official 5K at the end. Along the way, they also teach self-esteem, kindness, fighting bullying and a number of other super important life lessons. It's an amazing program and I've seen the positive effects it's had, not only on my daughters, but on all the girls who go through it.

I help my wife out at some of the events and am there every year as they run the 5K. Michele has a gift for working with these girls, a knack for bringing out the best in them and showing them they can accomplish any goal. One of the phrases she constantly repeats to them is, "You're stronger than you know." Every practice, every run, every 5K, she keeps telling them that. Reminding them that no matter what self-talk is going on in their head, no matter what anyone else might have told them, they are actually "stronger than they know."

I don't know if you're a runner, but starting from never running at all to running 3.1 miles in a couple of months is not that easy - especially with little seven-year-old legs. On day one of the program when the girls (and their parents) hear they'll be running that distance very soon, they all look back at Michele with concerned disbelief. Come race time though, every single girl crosses the finish line because, as it turns out, "they are all stronger than they know."

Watching their faces as they complete that distance for the first time, I can see that they too believe in themselves like they never have before. They now understand what they are capable of if they just apply themselves and stop telling themselves that they can't do it; they can do anything.

You, too, are stronger than you know. You are NOT average, so don't settle for average. Average sucks.

Just because you've never done something before doesn't in any way mean it can't be done. If someone else is doing it, so can you. All of us down here on planet Earth are more or less the same. Yes, it's true that some people have better resources or a more nurturing environment, but that only accounts for maybe 20% of it. The rest is grit, determination and belief.

It's truly amazing what you can accomplish if you just believe in yourself. Self-doubt is the #1 killer of dreams and is what's holding you back from your true potential. Everything starts with belief. Once you realize that you are stronger than you know, the next time you look up, you'll see that that ceiling you put on your capabilities was never really there at all.

"If you always put limits on everything you do, physical or anything else, it will spread into your work and into your life. There are no limits. There are only plateaus, and you must not stay there, you must go beyond them."

- Bruce Lee

This is perfectly illustrated by fleas. Yes, you read right, fleas. Let me share the tale of the flea with you so you don't make his mistakes.

As a dog guy, I'm not that fond of fleas. They are annoying and aggravatingly hard to get rid of once your pet is infested with the little bastards. At the same time, they are also very impressive. Fleas are one of best jumpers in the animal world (second only to froghoppers, in case it ever comes up on trivia night) and have the ability to jump up to 7.9 inches high. That may not seem like much, but when you consider that's an impressive 50 times their body length, you gotta give the little guys credit.

What's interesting is that, if you put a flea in a small jar - say four inches tall - and screw the lid on him, he will start jumping like crazy, hitting his tiny head repeatedly on the lid. After a period of time, the flea would learn that he can't escape the jar and stop jumping so high and cracking his noggin. Then if you take the lid off, the flea will continue to jump at the height just short of four inches. Even though he would have no problem getting out of the jar, he doesn't try because he's put that limit of four inches on himself. Since he BELIEVES he will never escape, he stops trying. He's failed so many times that he's given up. He's put the limit on his abilities and never bothers to look up to see if the lid is even there. He assumes he can't do it, so he can't and will stay trapped in the jar as long as you want to keep the little dude there.

You, too, may be living with a lid on your life. A lid that you put there and that is really just an illusion. Let me give you some breaking news; you are lidless, my friend. There is no ceiling to your life and no limit to what you can do. So jump and keep jumping. Yes, you're going to hit your head sometimes - probably more than you'd like - just don't let it stop you from jumping. Life in the jar is boring. That's where the average fleas hang out. Don't be that flea! You have so much more in store for you than a life within a small jar.

I have one more metaphorical animal story to drive this home to hopefully make you realize you need out of Averagetown, ASAP. This one is about lobsters (fleas and lobsters?! - I know, where did all the dogs go?) This crustacean fable was first told to me by my good buddy, Patrick, and is another example of how our human traits can also be found in the animal kingdom. Listen up and see if you can identify when this has happened in your life. It's called "lobster syndrome".

If you've ever been to a fine seafood restaurant, you may have noticed the tank of fresh, live lobsters there. You'll also notice that the walls of the tank are not all that tall. In fact, a lobster could pretty easily climb out if he tried. So why don't the lobsters all storm the walls and make a break for it?

It's not that they are incapable of doing so - they are. If you put only one lobster in such a tank he will climb out pretty quickly and be free. It's only when you have more than one that they are unable to get out, and it's all due to that pesky lobster syndrome. It keeps the lobsters from freedom every single time and might be seriously holding you back as well.

When you have a group (two or more) of lobsters in a tank, and one ambitious fellow attempts to jump the wall, the other lobsters will quickly grab him and drag him back down. They will not allow him to escape, dooming them all to confinement. Human beings do this as well. Some people can't stand to see others succeed, either consciously or unconsciously. They want to keep those around them at the bottom with them and will do anything they can to pull you down, keeping you at their level so you can all be miserable together. It's sad, but if you think about it, I'm sure you can identify a few people in your life who are like this.

It is usually caused by their own insecurities and short comings. If they see others doing well, it makes them feel badly about themselves, so they sabotage you, which makes them feel a little better. Misery loves company. Many times they do this in a very subtle, passive aggressive way that you might not even notice and, if you're not careful, they will totally derail your aspirations and potential.

It might be a quick negative comment about a new opportunity you have, talking you into thinking that something is just not possible or planting seeds that break your confidence. Whatever they do, it's always to keep you from doing what they can't, escaping where they're stuck or preventing you from becoming better than they are.

It's critical to your success and happiness that you identify any potential lobsters in your life, see them for what they are and not allow them to pull you down or hold you back from escaping to a better life. They could be co-workers, friends or even close family members. Don't take what they say or do personally - it's not about you, it's about them. You just need to become immune to their nonsense so that it doesn't affect your progress.

Which leads us to taking a good, hard look at your inner circle ...

16

Your Inner Circle

I arrived on the Seton Hall University campus full of nervous excitement. This would be my first of four years at the college and I really wasn't sure what to expect. I didn't particularly like high school all that much - well at least not the last two years.

In the summer between tenth and eleventh grade, we moved from the small town of Leonia, where I had grown up, to Clifton, which was huge. Although both were in New Jersey, the two towns couldn't be more different. Leonia was a quiet place where everyone in town knew each other and, having lived there since I was four years old, it was my entire world. Clifton was a more culturally diverse town with so much more activity and happenings.

As you might imagine, the move was very challenging for me, a shy, insecure kid, who was totally intimidated with my new surroundings. That first September, I was the new kid, lost in a sea of 2,200 high school students (to give you some perspective, Leonia High School had around 650 total students) who already had friends and didn't care too much about letting some stranger into their circles. In the beginning, I ate many lunches alone and felt very out of place.

After a while I was able to make a few friends and survive my last two years of high school. However, I never really enjoyed my time at Clifton High and counted the days until I got my diploma and escaped. The dramatic change of moving probably contributed to me becoming a little depressed, but was not the only factor leading to my poor attitude in my adolescence.

Back in Leonia, I was a bit of a pessimistic little boy. I had a great childhood there, filled with long summer days playing outside with a great group of friends. We lived in an apartment complex on a dead end street and I was in the last unit, tucked away in the back. It was a safe and friendly community which allowed me the freedom to romp with my brother and buddies from sun up until dinner time.

My best friend growing up was named John, who lived three doors down from me. I'm not sure how it happened or which one of us was responsible for it, but we both had pretty negative outlooks. Our favorite phrase when anything didn't go remotely our way was that we got "dicked over."

I don't think that either of us were the source of the negativity, but rather, it was fed by both of us, causing us to become bitter and always expecting things to not go our way (at which we would say, we got "dicked over" again). That gray foundation was ignited by my move to Clifton and expanded my negativity to new levels as I entered my first college year.

At Seton Hall I was paired up with my first and last roommate, Mark. Even though we had never met until that first day freshman year, we become great friends and continued to room together for the rest of our college years (and he continues to be one of my best friends today). I started that first year with a pretty grim outlook.

I was easily defeated and played a never-ending soundtrack of negative self-talk in my head.

I wasn't all gloom and doom though. I had a tremendous amount of fun as well. I quickly found a great group of friends and thoroughly enjoyed the college social life (academics, not so much). Even though I had my share of fun, there was still an underlying persistent depression that would remain for my entire college career. It was always there and would surface every so often, causing me to sit in my room alone in the dark. I think my poor attitude even started to rub off on Mark, who seemed to be getting sucked into my melancholy.

Looking back now, I see that if things had continued like this my life would have probably taken a much darker path. Luckily for me, as I started my freshman year in college, someone came into my world who dramatically changed the trajectory of my life.

It wasn't this thing that happened instantaneously, and I didn't have an "aha" moment where I saw my mistakes and changed everything overnight. No, this was a gradual shift that took years to complete. Even though it took a long time for the effects to be noticed and my transformation from depressed kid to the outgoing, confident, happy adult I am today would require years of personal development and self-work to complete, I know that this one person was the one that made it all possible.

The cool thing here is that he didn't set out to make me a better person and actually had no idea that he was even influencing me - he was just being himself. His name is Jeff. Although we had both gone to Clifton High School together and sort of knew each other from playing on the basketball team there, it wasn't until we both started at Seton Hall that we began regularly hanging out.

Jeff was the total opposite of me back then. He was happy, fun, super outgoing and overflowing with confidence. His personality was such a contrast to mine, it's a wonder that we ever become friends. It might be because Jeff wasn't at all judgmental, or because he was a commuter and I was a resident on campus and he needed a place to crash after parties. Either way, I'm so grateful that he came into my life and that he remains a good friend today.

Just hanging around Jeff and seeing his amazing attitude and watching how he lived his life was the antidote I needed to break my downward spiral of negativity and show me there was another (more fun) alternative. The more I hung out with him, the more the seeds of change dug into my subconscious.

It's not so much that Jeff turned things around for me, but more that he stopped me from continuing on the path I was on. He was a bubbling example of how life could and should be lived. He was always upbeat, with a smile on his face and expected things to go his way, instead of waiting to get "dicked over". It was so refreshing and made me start to realize that there was another way to do things.

Jeff was also the first person who made me rethink failure. As a shy, insecure teenager, the very thought of talking to a girl made me sweat and want to curl into a fetal position. What if she didn't like me? What if she rejected me? Aghhhhhhhh! Jeff didn't think that way. Instead he thought, what if she does like me? What if she wants to go out with me? His confidence was unwavering

- no matter how beautiful the girl, he was never intimidated or dissuaded.

The impressive thing is that his superior attitude didn't stop Jeff from getting rejected - I watched many girls turn him down (sometimes embarrassingly). What I loved the most is that it NEVER seemed to affect him, kill his mood or slow him down one bit. He shook it off like water off a duck's back. He never, ever let a single failure define him or stop him from trying. Jeff just moved on, expecting the next girl to be happy to talk to him. It was amazing to watch and really opened my eyes to a totally new way of thinking.

Always keep in mind with whom you spend your time will greatly affect what you believe and who you become.

Upon reflecting on my life now, I can see how those around me profoundly affected my thinking and swayed my actions, sometimes for the good, and other times, not so much. You need to be very intentional about who gets your ear and is let into your head because, like it or not, they are influencing you.

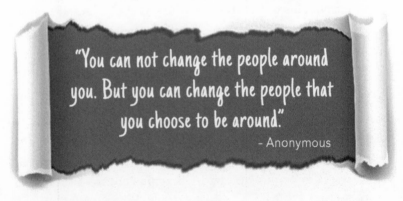

"You can not change the people around you. But you can change the people that you choose to be around."
- Anonymous

Personal development great, Jim Rohn, said that and he's right on the money. Who are the people around you? Are they positive influences or could they be exposing you to negative thinking?

If all those around you are downers (like young me), you'll tend to think that way too. But if you surround yourself with upbeat Jeffs, life will be very different. Make a list of the five people you spend the most time with and write down if they are positive thinkers or negative nellies. Are they happy or miserable? Are they successful or are they going nowhere?

This stuff matters - big time. You will always tend to default to the average outcomes of those around you. Now, I'm not saying you have to get rid of all your friends and stop spending time with your family if they don't fit the bill, but it does mean you might want to rethink how much time you're spending with them and upgrade your inner circle.

When I finally realized this law (and I do believe it's a natural law), I had to cut a few toxic people out of my life that were just not serving me and limit the time I spent with some friends and family who were not positive influences. At the same time, I sought out to create new relationships with people who inspire me.

When I first started doing this, I looked locally for people who were in my area. But now, thanks to technology, you can increase your inner circle online. One of the things I love the most about The FernDog Trainer Academy is our private Facebook group and monthly coaching calls. We have such an amazing group of students (both past and present) from all over the world who all work together to motivate and inspire one another. You need to seek out and put people in your life that will lift you up and help you move toward the life you really want for yourself.

Jeff was so much more than a good friend to me back then, he was my very first mentor. I didn't realize it at the time, but he was pulling out the weeds of negativity growing in my head and planting seeds of positive change that would soon start to sprout, leading me toward the life I now lead.

Find people that can lift you higher and that you aspire to be like and get them into your life. If you're like me (and I'm guessing you are), you want to be happy, fulfilled, positive and successful, so surround yourself with these kinds of people and influences.

My hope is that, by reading this book, I can be one of your new mentors and that these words will be one of the defining points in your life where your life's trajectory turns to a slightly more positive direction.

Keep reading . . . we have more weeds to pull and more seeds to plant.

17

Stubborn Refusal
to Quit

I heard the crash as I reached the bottom of the stairs and turned my body toward the kitchen, and my heart sank immediately. I knew that my Pit Bull, Hayley, had not been far behind me as I hurried down the stairs and knew what that the crash meant. Hayley was 14 years old, which is pushing the limits on the typical lifespan of these types of dogs. Although she was in relatively sound health for an old lady, she did suffer from arthritis in her back legs and partial hip dysplasia.

I quickly turned around and saw her sprawled out on the hardwood floor at the bottom of the stairway. Ever loyal, when I started down the stairs, she followed as usual. However, her achy legs couldn't keep up, and down she tumbled. I rushed to her side, flooded with worry, knowing what a fall like this could do to a dog of her age. She was alive but dazed and not moving.

After a few moments, the spark reappeared in her eyes and she tried to stand. She got her front legs up but her back legs were unresponsive causing her to collapse once again. Not deterred, Hayley tried again, but the back half of her body just hung lifeless and down she went. We watched as she did this a few more times, trying so hard to rise but never able to get her back legs to offer her much support.

During this ordeal, Hayley never made a sound - she just persistently kept trying to stand, ignoring the incredible pain she must have been experiencing. I was sure that she had broken her back legs and that this was the end. My wife was crying and I was heartbroken.

I called my vet and let him know what had happened and that I would be bringing Hayley in immediately. Before I left with her, I had my daughters say goodbye, assuming this would be the last time they ever saw her. Even now, years later, the image of this scene in my mind makes my eyes well up.

At the vet's office, Hayley still couldn't stand but seemed alert. After looking her over and assessing the options, the vet decided to give her some pain medications and recommended we see what happens over the next 24 hours. I was emotionally drained and slightly relieved that there was a chance she might make it through this, but didn't really think she would ever have use of her back legs again.

She slept soundly that night, thanks to the medications, and the next day woke up and once again tried to stand up. Even after a good night's sleep, she wasn't able to get her back legs underneath her and, once again, Hayley was unaffected by her lack of success and continued to try over and over for the next hour. It hurt me so much to see her like this and, as I looked on as she repeatedly fell, I considered that I shouldn't allow her to live like this - it just wasn't fair to her. Then the unimaginable happened - she got up.

It wasn't pretty and she looked incredibly unstable, but she was up. Over the next few days she improved slowly and was eventually able to walk again, albeit wobbly. I was so relieved and utterly amazed at her perseverance and determination. I can't imagine the pain she must have always been in, but never once did she complain (in contrast to my current Beagle who yelps like he's being tortured if he steps on a pebble) or stop trying.

Hayley proved to me what can be accomplished if you're properly motivated and not to let setbacks stop you from continuing to try again. Although Hayley never did stairs again (I carried her up and down), we were rewarded with two additional, good years with her.

I often think back to my Hayley girl when I take a fall in life and am tempted to just give up. I think, "What would Hayley do?" and the answer is always the same: push aside the pain and get up. Then, keep getting up until you succeed. This has served me well over the years because I seem to be very prone to falling down. I've had countless failures that have made me question my abilities and consider giving up, but I think of Hayley and keep on trying.

Many times, people quit right before they are about to succeed, and if they just pushed through for a little longer, they would have made it. The problem is we get discouraged easily and can let the lack of initial success totally derail us. In a world full of instant gratification, we expect things to happen fast - and when it doesn't, we think it never will.

Patience is not easy. Historically, I'm not a terribly patient guy. However, over the years, I've learned to control my gut reaction to bail on things early and persevere to see things through. It's still not easy and I'm still a work in progress, but I've had some experiences that have taught me it can pay to stick things out. It takes conscious will power and practice because the easy thing to do is to quit. It's hard to keep going when nothing's going according to plan. However, if you really believe in what you're doing, you owe it to yourself to give it every opportunity to succeed.

Almost everything doesn't go perfect out of the gate, and often, things can be pretty crappy before it all turns around. So many success stories out there begin with lots of hardships, failures and setbacks, but the people involved kept going in spite of all the difficulties and were able to fight through them and make their dreams come true. It's not easy - if it were, everyone would be a huge success at everything they tried. The reality is that to accomplish something great, you need to understand that it's a process which is very often challenging as you experiment and learn the best way to do it.

There are very few "overnight successes". Most of the time you only see the end result but not all the work that came before the triumph. You may see me with a thriving dog training business with lots of opportunity, but don't realize that to get here I had to overcome a ton of obstacles, multiple failures and seemingly devastating problems along the way. When my students learn of some of the things I had to go through to get to where I am now, they finally understand the journey was not all puppy kisses and piles of money. But, if you hang in there, keep picking yourself up and learning from your mistakes, success can be inevitable.

"The difference between winning and losing is most often not quitting."

- Walt Disney

The only difference between a successful person and an unsuccessful person is that one gave up and the other kept going - even when times got tough. This doesn't mean that you should be moving forward on everything. Some projects and ideas are not good ones or may not be possible. There's a very blurry line between what you should keep trying at after a large number of failures and what you should scrap. I believe if something is really important to you, you need to keep going - especially if it's been done before by others. And if it's never been done before, it doesn't mean you can't do it. It just means you have to really have a good understanding of what you're trying to do and have the data showing it can be done.

For example, if I decided my goal was to play professional basketball at my current age of 48, with my mediocre (at best) hoops skills, I don't think there's any amount of perseverance that is going to get that to happen for me. It's unrealistic and probably a goal I should give up on. I could give it a good go, but eventually I would have to come to terms with the reality of the situation - I'm a bit too old (my body would not be able to physically handle the demands) to play professional basketball and it would take me years and years of practice to get good enough to increase my skill level to be able to compete. Oh well, no NBA for me.

Keep in mind that, just because no one has ever done something before, doesn't mean you can't do it. If you truly believe in what you're trying to accomplish, combined with a burning desire to see it successful, then you need to keep going, no matter how many times you hit a dead end.

When Henry Ford came up with the idea to build his now famous V-8 engine, every single engineer he had working for him told him it was impossible to build an eight cylinder engine in a single block. Ford's response was, "Produce it anyway." He knew it could be done and, even though no one else on his team (or elsewhere) thought it would ever happen, Ford didn't care. It was his passion to get it done. Time and time again, his engineers tried to build it but with no success. Every time they came back empty handed, Ford would tell them to keep trying. After many failures, the engineers were able to find a way to make it work, much to the surprise of everyone except Henry Ford.

When I just started as a dog trainer, I can remember hustling so damn hard to get my name out there, build some business relationships and get some paying clients. I was driving all over to local businesses, working the crowd in dog parks, as well as blogging and posting videos online. I was working long hours, seven days a week, but still wasn't seeing many results from all my efforts. I was so frustrated and many times questioned if this was a good idea and that maybe I should just pack it in and give up.

Although it looked bleak, I never gave up and boy am I glad I didn't. It was hard to keep going day after day, with no measurable perceived progress, but I knew I really wanted to be a dog trainer and really believed I could be good at it. I just had to keep going. I didn't let anything deter me from my dream. I kept getting up, day after day, falling down and getting back up again. Eventually all my hard work paid off and success came. It was in no way easy but well worth the effort.

For the last five years or so, I've been an avid podcast listener. I think it's a great way to learn some new things while you're driving, walking the dog or just have some free time. When I decided to create an online business for myself to supplement my dog training (I needed something I could do while still being able to watch my kids at home), I found a great podcast called Internet Business Mastery. On the show, the hosts, Jason Van Orden and Jeremy Frandsen, talk about a wide variety of topics designed to help launch an online business.

I probably listened to over 100 episodes of that show. They were packed full of great, actionable info and both Jason and Jeremy are very likable and honest. Although I can't remember a lot of the specifics about the things I heard, I've implemented countless ideas and strategies that I learned there.

There's one particular line that I heard on the podcast that stands out for me above everything else. The guys were discussing what the secrets were to their personal successes, and Jeremy said something that immediately got tattooed on my brain. He said the main reason he has been able to have a successful online business is his "stubborn refusal to quit."

I love that quote and try to live it every day with the things that are the most important in my life. There will be so many factors -

people in your life, external forces pushing against you and/or sheer exhaustion. However, if you really want something bad enough and have a "stubborn refusal to quit," you will get there eventually.

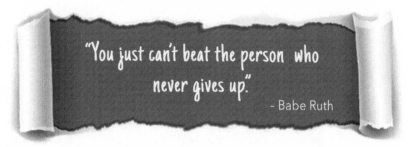

"You just can't beat the person who never gives up."

- Babe Ruth

18

Putting Yourself Out There

"Do you want me to set you up with her?"

The question caught me off guard. I was getting my hair cut in a local salon not far from my house. Michelle, my hairdresser, had become a friend over the years and knew much of my personal life (as most hairdressers do), including my not so recent break up with my last girlfriend. Every month and a half when I came in to get my hair cut, Michelle and I would catch up with each other's lives and chat while she turned my overgrown brown hair into something appealing.

Over the last six months, Michelle had heard me talk about how my girlfriend had broken up with me unexpectedly, shattering my fragile heart into a million pieces, followed by my summer of self-destruction and misery, culminating into my present state of mild acceptance with a side of bitterness. During the half year since my break up, Michelle had listened and supported me as good friends do. I had come in to get my hair cut a number of times, and although there was a single friend of hers also working at the salon doing nails, she never thought about getting us together because she could see I wanted nothing to do with another relationship. This day, however, I seemed different to her. My mood seemed brighter and, out of nowhere, her friend, who was in the other room giving a pedicure, came to mind and she thought we might make a good match.

She told me a little about her and asked if I would like to meet her. Immediately my emotional defense mechanism activated in attempt to spare me anymore heartache. My last experience with a girl ended tragically, spiraling me into a miserable place that just plain sucked. I had no plans on going through that again. It was much easier to just keep myself protected and away from all relationships. That way I would never get hurt like that again.

But what if . . .

What if she didn't whack away at my heart like a piñata? What if things were different this time? What if she was awesome?

It was hard to know if I should take such a chance again, given what happened the last time. All these thoughts ricocheted around my head while Michelle waited for my response in mid-snip of my hair. I knew that if I never got back out there, this was as good as my life would get - romantically at least. Although I could live a pretty good life alone, I knew I was craving more.

"Sure," I said. "I'll meet her."

Michelle brought me into the back room where her friend (also named Michele - but with one "l") was working and gave us a super quick and very awkward introduction. I just said hi, she said hi and Michelle whisked me back out, where she asked me what I thought of her. I didn't have much time to really get anything but a quick glance, but was able to ascertain that she was indeed attractive and seemed nice enough, so I gave her the green light to hook us up.

The next week we all met out together at a local restaurant/ bar for a few drinks, followed by an official first date, followed by another, then another and more after that. Long story short, I ended up marrying that Michele and we now have an amazing family and life together.

I'm *so* glad I decided to take the risk and put myself out there again. Shaking off my past hurt and being willing to meet someone new, despite what happened the last time I got involved with someone, totally changed my life for the better.

"Sometimes things fall apart so that better things can fall together."
- Marilyn Monroe

You'll also find that the more you do, the more you try, the more you put your fear aside and see what will happen, the more good things will happen to you. That doesn't mean nothing bad will happen, because it occasionally will. You might get your feelings hurt and sometimes your heart may break a little, but you can't let that possibility stop you from taking another chance because your past experience doesn't guarantee the same for your future attempts.

I see so many people missing out on things because they stay with what they know - afraid to see what's out there in the unknown. You've heard the expression, "If you just keep doing what you've always done, you'll get what you've always gotten." To get more you have to do more. That can sometimes be scary, but let me assure you there is so much more out there for you. You just need to go find it.

I'm constantly challenging my students in The FernDog Trainer Academy to put themselves out there by creating content, meeting people and doing more. I've learned that the more you do, the more opportunities will come your way (seemingly out of nowhere). I push them to create online videos, write blogs, post on social media and network with businesses around them. Almost all of them are scared and reluctant to put themselves out there at first, afraid of rejection and possible embarrassment.

As I've put myself out there personally and professionally, I've gotten both rejected and embarrassed many times, but I've also had some pretty incredible things happen as well. I was very nervous (especially in the beginning) about making videos and posting them online for the world to see. They didn't always work out well but I've gotten so much business as a result.

When I first started blogging, it was nerve racking. People didn't always agree with my point of view and some people were just downright nasty. I kept it going though, and after I had been blogging for a few years, I was contacted by a company that had stumbled upon my website, liked my writing and hired me to write for them. The job lasted for a year and paid me very well, all because they saw the content I had put out. Remember that speaking gig at Rutgers University I told you about earlier? The reason the director of the Animal Science Department invited me to speak to the students was because she saw one of my videos online.

These are just two of the countless opportunities that have "fallen into my lap" just because I put myself out there. The more you do, the more cool stuff will happen to you. I'm always doing new things and, because of this, new things are constantly happening to me. Yes, it's scary sometimes and yes, you're often making things up as you go, but that's fine. The key to make it work out in a favorable way is to always be providing value. Don't do anything for the sole purpose of getting something in return - that will rarely work. Just do your best to help people and put out the best stuff you can and you will get noticed.

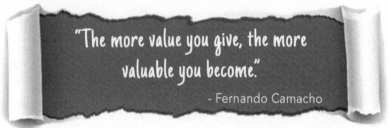

"The more value you give, the more valuable you become."

- Fernando Camacho

The biggest thing that holds people back from putting themselves out there is caring too much about what other people think. You have to let go of that. Who cares what other people think? Why does that matter so much to you? Did you ever really think about it? Probably not, but you should.

Here's the deal, not everyone is going to like you and agree with you . . . and that's okay (it's actually normal and to be expected). If you let the opinions of others stop you, you're being held captive by your own mind and it's stopping you from getting what you want. This means developing a little bit of a thick skin for criticism.

When I first started blogging and posting on social media, if I got one negative comment, I would be sick over it for a week or more. I would let it eat away at me and let it stop me from creating more content for fear of others disagreeing with me. Over time, I realized the truth. No matter what you're doing or talking about, there are going to be some people who agree and like it and others who will hate it. I learned that it's actually good to stand up for what you believe and cause people to make a choice; they either connect with my message or they don't. Either way, I'm cool with it. Whoever likes me can come over here and all those who don't, can go way over there and do their thing.

If you try to satisfy everyone, you'll end up diluting what you want to accomplish, which will greatly hamper your results. Decide on what's important to you and then start putting yourself out there. It's better to identify everyone who's not on the same page as you so you know who you shouldn't waste your time focusing on. When you come across some haters, don't take it so personally (even though they may say some personal stuff to you). Ultimately, their words and actions are not so much about you and more about their own issues.

Now I get excited when there are some people disagreeing with me. It means I took a stand. I chose my side and those who are with me will rally to my cause and I don't really care about the others - they are not my people. I wish them well and that's it - I let them and their opinions go.

A year or so ago I wrote a blog post that I knew would get some people all fired up and mad at me. The post was called, "Why Retractable Leashes Are Bad for Your Dog." In the blog article I said, very boldly, why I think retractable leashes are horrible and recommended that people throw them in the garbage. I got more negative comments and messages for that post than any other I've ever written. Did I mind? No. It actually made me happy because that's what I expected to happen. I knew some people wouldn't like my opinion about those leashes and would let me know (and boy did they).

All in all I probably got about ten or so angry responses to that post. On the flip side, it also set a record for the most positive comments I've received and it was shared on Facebook just under three thousand times. That post helped me get more followers and people over to my website than any other post to date. I took my stand, took a few punches and reaped the rewards. If I was afraid of what people would say, I wouldn't have been able to ever push the publish button, which would have limited me from getting all the great exposure that came from it.

The more you put yourself out there, the more haters will surface. Expect them but don't worry about them or let them stop you. Pick your goals, find your message and then keep putting yourself out there.

Putting yourself out there also means trying new things. If you want more out of life, you need to keep trying more things. I like to think of everything as an experiment. If you keep doing the same things year after year, life will never change or get better. Life should be a constant evolution where you're growing a little more with every turn of the calendar. So, every year, I strive to try some new things I've never done before. This is part of my business success strategy.

When one of my students reaches out to me because his or her dog training business isn't growing, I always start by asking if this year is any different/better than last year. If they come back and say their business is kind of the same as it was last year, I immediately ask, "What are you doing differently this year?" After some back and forth, we find out they aren't really doing anything differently this year. They're just continuing with the same plan over and over.

My "brilliant" coaching advice for them is to start doing some new things - to put themselves out there in different ways. They need to try new approaches and techniques to keep moving their business forward.

Be brave, be bold and keep putting yourself out there. Who knows, you might just end up with a wife or husband because of it.

19

It's Time for an Upgrade

I was leaning against a tall shelf against the outside wall of Bar Anticipation, an outdoor bar in one of the many beach towns along the New Jersey coast. If you live in Jersey, you go "down the shore" every chance you can from Memorial Day to Labor Day - it's one of the unwritten laws of The Garden State.

This particular day was gorgeous - warm but not crazy hot as the sun dipped low on the horizon. My friends and I gathered at this bar every year at this time for Seton Hall Young Alumni Day. Bar A (as it's called) ran a special day for some of the New Jersey Colleges where recent graduates could catch up with old classmates and take advantage of some yummy drink specials. This was our fifth year attending and it was getting obvious that we were pushing the envelope on the definition of "young alumni."

I was hanging out with my buddies, reminiscing about old times, when one of our old acquaintances from school spotted us from across the bar and strolled over to say hi. I hadn't seen him since graduation but it was like not a day went by. We exchanged a friendly hug, after which he steps back and remarks on my physique, which took him a bit by surprise.

In college (and for all my life prior) I had been built like a shoe lace - tall, lanky and loose. After graduation, I joined a gym and discovered I loved working out. Combine that with proper nutrition, and I had seen some nice results and was in pretty good shape. You wouldn't confuse me for *The Rock* but my tall frame was now lean and muscular.

My long lost amigo looked me over and said, "Damn, I wish I looked that good. You're so lucky."

I smiled and changed the subject, still not comfortable handling compliments (inside I was still the insecure string bean.) Later though, I thought about the exchange and wished I told him the truth . . . that luck had nothing to do with it.

I didn't just wake up one day with a different body, I worked my ass off to get it. While he was sleeping late, watching hours of TV or hanging out at this very bar, I was at the gym putting in the work. I made getting in shape a priority, did the work and got the results (funny how that works). Since then, I've continued to make physical fitness a priority and, although I'm not as ripped as I was in my late 20's, I remain pretty fit.

Working out was the start of my total transformation. I started out a shy, insecure, skinny, moderately depressed kid who is now a confident, healthy, happy adult who's loving every single day. Today I'm a totally different person than I used to be back at Seton Hall University. My wife finds it hard to believe because she only knows this guy. If she met me back then, she never would have bothered with a second date. With every single workout my confidence grew. As my body changed, I felt better about myself and it started to change my inner dialog, which in turn had ripple effects on every aspect of my life.

That was the beginning for me. I started with my body but then, years later, finally realized that in all my workouts, I had been neglecting the most important body part - my mind. My external improvements had sparked the beginnings of inner change, but unless I concentrated my efforts on working on mental wellbeing, my improved attitude would be fleeting. To truly transform into the best version of myself, I would need to get serious and put in the same amount of time and effort into beefing up my inner self that I did on improving my body.

It wasn't until fifteen years after I began my physical fitness that I started consistently working on my mental health. If only I knew then what I know now. Working on what's inside is so much more important than working on your outside.

In my formal education as a personal trainer and my personal experimentation in fitness, I learned the surprising truth that most of your overall health and wellbeing come from your diet. What you put in your body has the biggest impact on how you look and feel (much more than exercise). Once I started working on my mind, I realized that this was so much more important to your overall wellbeing than the physical exercise. The ultimate way to have the very best life is to work on both the physical and mental sides of yourself.

So, what do I mean by "working on your mind"? Basically, it's learning to control your thoughts more effectively, understand what's going on in your head and design your thinking so that it's serving your ultimate purpose, to be happy. That's really why I was working out so hard. I wanted to feel better about myself and have a happier life. To accomplish that, I would need to focus on the root of why I was shy, insecure and depressed. The answers were not in my outward appearance but trapped within my head.

As soon as I started to read some personal development books and really observe my own thought patterns, I quickly saw where my problems were. I was in a subconscious cycle of negativity. I was constantly pessimistic and down on myself, which led straight to my insecurities. Once I realized I had been self-sabotaging my success and happiness for years, I made it my mission to change things and move forward.

I always tell my clients that everything with their dog is all repetitions, consistency and forming habits. The reason your dog continues to exhibit most of his behaviors is because it's become a habit over time. Once enough repetitions are done, it makes no difference why something started. The only reason it continues is it's become an involuntary habit. So you need to be very aware of what repetitions are being done because you're stuck with those habits, for good or for bad. The longer your dog has been doing a behavior, say barking out the window, the harder and more time consuming it will be to break the habit and reshape a new, more desirable behavior. That's why we need to be VERY aware of the repetitions being done.

The same is true for us. Reading one self-help book will not override decades of negative self-talk. For me, I was trying to reprogram a mental pattern that's been going on for most of my life. The first book was just a spark of change - a glimmer of what could be. To effectively change the way I thought, I was going to need a lot more repetitions. Since I first read "Think and Grow Rich" back in 2009, I've been doing daily repetitions of positivity and productive mental enrichment and the effects have been life changing.

If I've lost you here and you're thinking this is all just psycho babble BS, I completely understand, because that's exactly what I used to think as well. For years, my dad has been giving me some kind of personal development book every Christmas and every single year I used to smile, thank him and put it in the closet and forget about it. It wasn't until after my mind was open to the idea that I went into the closet and started reading through those books. Turns out, my dad knew what I was missing and had been trying to help me for years but I didn't see it and I couldn't accept his help until I was ready for it.

Your success in life will not be complete without this mental piece in place. You may be able to achieve personal or financial wins, but to enjoy long-term happiness and fulfillment, you can't skip this part because it's actually the most important part of the equation. People mistakenly think that once they obtain some outward goal (like losing twenty pounds or getting that promotion or making a certain amount of money) that they will then be happy. However, it's precisely the opposite.

One of my favorite books (and one I re-read every year or two) is "The Happiness Advantage" by Shawn Achor. In the book, Achor proves why this old formula for happiness is broken and shows how we must first learn to be happy BEFORE we'll ever find long-term success. He goes over the research that supports this and then details a road map to reprogram our brains to be more positive, which will bring more success in work and life. The book helped to open my eyes further on my own inner mistakes and create a new plan that would better serve me.

The reason why working on your mental attitude is so important is that, whether you know it or not, you're training the world on how to treat you. If you don't think much of yourself, neither will others. If you don't love yourself, no one else will. You need to be your number one fan and expect the best out of the world. If you are confident and happy inside, it will show outside as well.

No matter what you do in life professionally - whether you're a dog trainer, a waiter, an accountant or factory worker - you are your own product. People are buying you. That's why you get hired for any job, they're buying you. So if you want to get paid more, be more appreciated and advance in any career, it would make sense to work on yourself to make you the best you possible. If you do that, good things will happen, no matter what position you have or job you're in.

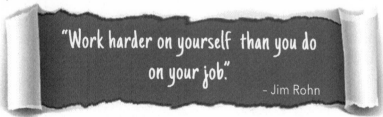

"Work harder on yourself than you do on your job."
– Jim Rohn

For the last eight years or so, I've made my personal improvement a high priority and have been doing daily repetitions to counter the gazillion reps of negative thinking I've done over the course of my life. You will always default to your past behavior patterns, so it's very important that you go out of your way to create some new, better repetitions that will better serve you. That's why I read so many books, listen to so many podcasts and watch so many videos, all on pretty much the same topics. I'm constantly reinforcing the beliefs I want my mind to adopt - I need lots of reps.

Much of the information I'm consuming I've already taken in before by another author, but that's cool. Different people say things in different ways and maybe the next book I read will present the same message I've heard before, but in a way that makes better sense to me. Or maybe, I wasn't ready to hear it quite yet and now I am.

Think about it, you don't do a bunch of pushups one time or go for a run once and see life changing results. You have to make exercise a regular part of your life and continue to do it to see the changes in yourself. The same is true of your mind. You can't attend one Tony Robbins seminar, get all fired up and then do nothing else and expect big changes to occur. You need to recondition your habits and your thinking, and to do that, you need continual repetitions of the message. Just like working your body out, it's hard in the beginning, but will get easier and require less effort as times goes on.

How you think will determine how you feel, and what you do will be the biggest influencer on the things that happen to you. If you allow negative messages to assault your brain, they will invade your mind like a greedy dictator and influence how you think. Unfortunately, most of the default messaging in the world is negative. Mainstream media is sensational by nature and if you're not careful, can flood you with accidents, conflicts and death. Is that what you want to let into your mind?

There are two times of day that your mind is most susceptible to influence: first thing in the morning and right before bed. When you get up in the morning, your mind has just "booted up" and is clear. It's like you're a computer that was just turned on and your desktop is empty with no open windows taking up bandwidth. Whatever you put in your mind first thing is likely to run in your background for the rest of the day. People who wake up and flick on the news are putting a virus into their operating system (am I taking this computer analogy too far?)

As you know, I start every single day by thinking of what I'm grateful for. It's a simple sixty second exercise that primes my day for positivity. If you wake up focusing on all the good in your life, you will more likely see the good life. Conversely, if you start your day with problems (yours or the world's) you'll likely see problems ahead.

A great way to supercharge your mind for the day is to follow up gratitude with ten (or more) minutes of reading something positive, a book, a magazine, a poem - anything that has a positive message. If you're not a reader, listen to an audio book or use an app like Peptalk (https://peptalkapp.com) to inject some positivity into your morning.

Here's my personal recipe that I use to prime my day for greatness. I get up at 6:00AM, an hour before my kids begin to stir, and as soon as I open my eyes in bed, I think of all the things I'm grateful for, then I take a quick shower, followed by ten to twenty minutes of meditation. Although I strongly believe in mediation, I'm not going to go into it here for fear of losing those who are just not ready for it. Just know that about 80% of successful high achievers, in a variety of fields, have some sort of meditation practice (according to "Tools of The Titans" by Tim Ferriss, another great read).

If you're looking for a good intro to meditation, I recommend picking up the book, "10% Happier" by Dan Harris. If meditation just isn't your thing, you can just sit quietly and think about how you want your day to go. What would make it great? This is setting your intention for the day.

After that, I schedule out my day, wake the kids, walk the dog and go into the world. This primes me for a great day. Now, just because you start off happy and positive doesn't mean life is going to cooperate and only give you roses and sunshine. Stuff is going to happen to you throughout the day that is going to attempt to derail your efforts of positivity. Starting your day off right won't change that. However, once you start doing it for a while, you'll discover that the stuff that happens won't affect you as strongly or for as long. Bad things won't sting as much and you'll rebound from them faster and with less of a struggle.

The key thing I want you to take away from all this is to be aware of how you're conditioning your mind. If you don't think about this and proactively input good stuff into your head, you'll get the default programming, which may not be serving you.

Want to know an easy happiness hack?

Smile. So simple, yet insanely powerful. Make it a habit to smile often. Not every minute, in every situation - that's a sure way to be labeled a loon - but in normal conversation. Smiling causes your brain to release dopamine, endorphins and serotonin, three neurotransmitters that make you feel good and help relieve pain (many anti-depressants contain these but you can get them free with no side effects!) Think of smiling as self-medicating. The more you smile, the better you will feel.

Smiling also makes you more likable to others. People inherently want to be around happy, cheerful people. Bonus! You'll make more friends and find people seeking out your company because when you smile, they smile more, which releases all that awesome brain juice for them, making them feel good. Just think, by smiling you could be causing a happiness chain reaction that goes on and on and on.

> "Sometimes your joy is the source of your smile, but sometimes your smile can be the source of your joy."
> - Thich Nhat Hanh

The last thing I want to bring to your attention is the language you use. Do you really pay attention to the things you say and their underlying feeling?

Most of us don't. We don't think about it at all, which means much of what comes out of our mouths is our conditioned responses, which is based on our default thinking. When I was a negative person, my normal responses were also negative and every time I said them, I reinforced them to myself - another negative repetition. To help change your thinking from negative to positive, you have to change what you regularly say.

Here's a common example. Someone says to you, "How are your today?" How you respond to them says a lot about what's going on inside your head. Let's look at some of the common responses:

"Fine" (said without thinking about the question at all) = I'm existing

"Hanging in there" = I'm barely surviving

"Another day, another dollar" = I hate my job

That's what you're telling yourself every time you say those things, and those are not the repetitions to being happy.

Like everyone else, I also tend to answer that question without thinking about it. However, I've reconditioned my response. I used to say all three of the above, but once I became aware of my language, I changed my responses and now I have a new default response to that question.

When someone asks me, "How are you?" I immediately reply, "Awesome!" I don't just state it, I say it enthusiastically. The more I do it, the better I feel. I'm training my thinking and my subconscious thoughts one response at a time. It's a simple thing that may seem trivial, but it can really help facilitate your change from a negative default to a positive one.

I've been subtly programming this into my daughters. Every day, on our short drive to school, I ask them what kind of day they're going to have. In the beginning they would give me some halfhearted version of "fine." I explained to them that this was unacceptable and that we wanted more than an average day, didn't we? They agreed we did, so I introduced them to a new expectation for the day. Now, whenever I ask them what kind of day they are going to have, they respond with, "Epic!" It's a small win in my fight to condition them to positivity, but a nice piece in the overall puzzle.

So, the next time someone asks you, "How are you?" I want you to respond with, "Awesome!" and see how it makes you feel. Then, keep it up, along with the language you use in other situations. The more you replace any negative talk with positive messaging, the more reps you'll be doing and the more effect it will have on you. on. At the very least, try to limit as much negative language as you can while trying to up the positive words you use on a regular basis.

Before long, you will have reprogrammed your default thinking to something that will lead to more happiness which, in turn, will bring you more success in every area of your life.

20

Dealing with Competition

It was beautiful day for an outdoor event. It was a late spring morning and all the vendors were setting up their areas within the park. The event was called Dogfest, a yearly festival where people came with their dogs to have some fun and maybe do a little shopping.

Although the location was a little out of my normal geographical range, it was early in my dog training career (maybe a year or two into it) and I wanted all the exposure I could get, so I had signed up as a vendor to promote my business. As I walked across the grassy field, I passed all kinds of dog-related businesses setting up their tables. There was a pet bakery stacking up neatly packaged yummy snacks, a booth filled with dog toys, collars and leashes, a stand with all kinds of dog related t-shirts, a local pet store and a variety of others that any dog lover would been drawn to.

After a seemingly long walk (long for someone carrying a folded long table, chair and overflowing backpack full of stuff), I arrived at my designated area. As I not so gently dropped the stuff in my hands on the ground, I exchanged smiles with the young woman in the spot to my right. She had gotten there earlier and had her table all set up and ready to go. She introduced herself cheerfully as Diane, a local dog trainer. As I started setting up my table, I happily informed her that I was also a dog trainer.

Her smile disappeared immediately and was replaced with a look of worry and stress. Her eyes darted left to right and seemed to be confused as to what to do or how to act. After a few moments, she composed herself and nervously asked where I was from. I told her and she quickly calculated the distance in her head, then let out a huge sigh of relief, "Oh, thank God! I thought you were another local trainer."

Now, I get that having two competing businesses side by side at the same event could be somewhat of a conflict. However, even if we were from the same town, I wouldn't have sweated it too much. Actually, I would have been fine with it for three reasons.

One, I honestly believe that I'm the best at what I do - even back then. Although I didn't have the amount of experience I have now, I still knew that I provided value to people and really felt I could help them better than any other dog trainer. It really doesn't matter to me how many trainers are around me. I have confidence in my abilities. I know who I am and the kind of help I can provide, and was eager to show it to the attendees of the festival once they arrived.

Secondly, if she was a better trainer or sales person than me, this would be a golden opportunity to watch and learn. I could see what she did well and use that information to help me in the future. I would also hope that by the end of the day we would be good friends and I would be able to pick her brain and get some guidance in the future. Something I would happily do for her if she asked.

The final reason I'm never threatened by competition is that if I worked all day, every day, forever I still wouldn't be able to take care of all the people and dogs that needed help. Here in the United States, there are 89.7 million dogs living in households. That's a lot of doggies and that number keeps going up every year. I don't have to worry about other dog trainers taking my business because there is plenty to keep us all busy for years to come.

> "You need to stop thinking competition and start thinking colleagues."
> – Fernando Camacho

All alone, you are limited. However, with the support of the other businesses around you, there's so much more you can accomplish. I'm friends with many of the dog trainers in my area. We share resources, help each other and even refer people to one another. If someone doesn't fit into my schedule, I'm not in their price range or I'm not the best fit for the issue they need solved, I'll send them over to one of my fellow trainers and they do the same for me. If I encounter a severe behavioral issue with a dog that I'm not comfortable addressing, I'll tell them about my buddy Ted. If someone is looking for a great puppy class, I send them over to Lynne. Then when someone is looking for advanced obedience, I refer them to Linda.

Students enrolled in my online course are located all over the globe. Since I can't be there in person, I recommend they seek out some local trainers to befriend and learn from. Sadly, most trainers refuse to help them because they feel threatened by them, afraid that if they teach them what they know, they'll swoop in and take all the business. This is very short-sighted thinking. There's so much we can accomplish together if we work together. I've collaborated on many projects with my fellow local trainers and it's always been an overwhelmingly positive experience.

The other big reason you should never be worried about your competition is that no one can be you. Although there are countless other dog trainers available in my area, none of them can be me. Part of my success is due to my skills as a dog trainer, but I'm sure one of the reasons people hire me is because of my personality and the way I communicate. This is why it's so important to constantly work on you. All that personal development we discussed earlier is critical to upping your awesomeness.

Since personalities are a very subjective thing, some people may like my personality while others will get turned off by it; there will be a chunk of the population that won't hire me because I'm me, and that's a good thing. I only want to work with people who are like-minded and appreciate similar things. I'm sort of goofy and like to make a lot of jokes, so someone who takes themselves very seriously is probably not going to like my style and I'm not really going to enjoy working with that kind of person as much. However, the people who are laid back and have a good sense of humor will be more attracted to me and I'll love having them as a client.

This is why it's so important to inject your personality into your business and promotional materials. You want to show everyone who you are so that you can immediately weed out those that are not the right fit and attract your ideal customers. Be yourself and know that you have cornered the market on you. No one else on the planet can copy that - it's all yours. By working hard on your dog training craft, combined with learning some business skills and developing everything about yourself, you become your biggest competitive advantage.

21

Redefining Wealth

I really felt sorry for him, sitting there all alone, eating his breakfast while he talked a bit too loudly on his cell phone trying to sound important. He was dressed in designer clothing and the waiters all seemed to know him so this was definitely not his first time at this high-end resort.

The view was just plain amazing. As my wife and I enjoyed our breakfast, we looked out of the big picture windows of the dining room to the partially frozen lake outside, glistening in the morning sun. This was our last day at The Mohonk Mountain House, a historic Victorian castle resort surrounded by 40,000 acres of pristine forest. We were there celebrating three special events: my wife's birthday, our anniversary and my birthday, all of which happen within two weeks of one another.

Although we always try to do something cool together around this time, staying at Mohonk was an extra special splurge this year. Normally, we would never be able to afford it, but we were able to get a special mid-week deal and had saved up for a while to make it happen. Even with the discounted price it was still more money than we typically spend on a two-day getaway, so we made sure we soaked up every single second.

The place is a cool combination of rustic beauty and upscale amenities, and my wife and I sampled as much as we could during our short stay. We went hiking around the lake (despite the chilly air), sat by the fireplace and indulged in some spa treatments, all while enjoying each other's company. As parents it can be hard to get away without the kids, but my wife and I do our best to sneak away for a weekend alone at least once a year. It's so important to reconnect without the chaos of everyday life to keep our relationship strong.

As I watched the old guy stabbing at his eggs all alone, I thought it was such a sad sight. We had met him and his very young (maybe 25 - 35 years younger) girlfriend yesterday while taking a mountain bike excursion on the trails around the resort. They were both a bit snooty and obviously lived a lifestyle that Michele and I couldn't quite relate to (I had to hear about his cashmere gloves more than once on our 45 minute bike ride.) Like us, they were here for a short getaway, but unlike us they didn't seem to really like each other all that much.

It was the off season for the resort (which is why we could afford it) and there was only a small amount of people there. The good part was that it was nice and quiet, the bad part was is we seemed to run into this couple everywhere we went. When Michele was in the women's lounge after a massage, she overheard the young girl telling the staff that she was hiding there from her partner, while I watched him on the men's side continually ask the staff if they had seen her.

Watching the two of them was like a bad reality show, the older rich dude and the over-the-top trophy girlfriend. Sometime during our first day there as the show unfolded in front of us, we decided to Google this guy and see what his deal was. According to the interwebs, he and his family owned a series of pawn shops throughout the Southeast United States. Our snooping confirmed what we suspected: he was crazy rich. Moving over to his Facebook profile, we saw that the young chicky he had with him was not a new thing. There were pictures of them together on a boat in the Mediterranean, at night clubs in Miami and on a whole slew of different beach resorts. Surprisingly, it seems like they were a thing.

I thought about all this as I had my breakfast that morning in Mohonk. Here was this guy who probably makes more money in a weekend than I make all year, and the only thing I felt for him was pity. He had the cash, the status, the young girl, the fancy clothes, expensive accessories but no one to eat with (even though he was "with" someone at this resort). I looked over at him and was struck by how sad his life was. On the surface he had everything, but where it really mattered, he was destitute.

Sitting there having breakfast with my loving wife, I was struck by how very rich I was and how sadly poor he was. I had everything that mattered and he had nothing that mattered. All his wealth was in material objects but he had nothing of substance in his life. On the surface, you might think he was living the good life. However, after observing the reality of his world, it was obvious to me that it was a hollow and lonely existence. Like so many, he had misunderstood what true wealth really was, focused on the wrong things and now was paying the price and eating alone. Sad.

It doesn't matter if your bank account is full as long as your heart is. Looking at him, I realized that I was the wealthy one. I had a fulfilling career I loved where I got to help both people dogs every single day, an amazing wife who loved me, to share my time with, great kids who would soon wrap their arms around me, telling me how much they missed me, thoughtful friends who would always be there when I needed them (not because of what I could do for them but because they cared about me), and a peaceful mind, content to appreciate the everyday blessings all around me. On the surface he had it all, but I was rich where it counted and, from where I was sitting, he was flat broke.

I invite you to redefine what you consider wealthy. Look beyond the superficial exterior and dig deep to find what's really important in life. We think we want lots of money, when what we really want is acceptance. We believe we need to be respected, when we really desire close relationships. We strive so hard for success and status, when all we really need is love.

Over the years, I've moved away from focusing on material gains and acquiring objects, to making sure I'm maximizing my time and enjoyment on a daily basis. It all comes down to understanding what's really important in life - and it's not possessions. So much of our society attempts to distract us from what really matters by seducing us with the quests for more stuff: nicer cars, bigger houses, swanky clothing, the newest iPhone, and on and on and on . . . when that's not what we should be using to gauge our success and happiness.

Our wealth does not come from stuff. Having all the money and all the gadgets in the world will not leave you feeling fulfilled (there's plenty of people in the public eye that have proved that.) Don't get me wrong, having lots of money and buying cool stuff is not bad - just don't expect those things to fill you up and create your happiness.

It's great to be ambitious and it's totally okay to want nice things, just don't get them at the expense of what's really important. If you're working long hours at a job you don't really like just to buy things you really don't need, you will never be happy. If your job keeps you away from your family while your kids are growing up without you, it's time to rethink what makes you (and them) happy.

> "Ask yourself what's really important, and then have the wisdom and courage to build your life around your answer."
> - Lee Jampolsky

What my family wants the most from me is my time. They don't care what we do, as long as we're doing it together. Remember, time is the most precious commodity on this planet. It's just about the only thing that you can't replenish.

I think of my time as an endangered species (told you, I'm an animal nerd) that has limited numbers and needs protecting. If you don't take measures to use your time well, it might be gone before you realize it. Treasure and value your time more than anything else in your life. Use it wisely and in ways that are designed to make you happy as much as possible.

I now engineer my life so that my time is used to bring me the most happiness, doing the things that bring me the most fulfillment. I am "squeezing the juice" out of life and making the most of all the days I have here. I still think big picture and long-term. However, I make sure that the things I do daily are not only making me happy in the moment, but also are fortifying my future happiness.

Focusing on the important things in life has made me a very wealthy man. I may only have a small house, drive an eleven-year-old car, wear plain clothes and don't go out to dinner much. However, I have a job I'm passionate about, a wife who loves me, two daughters I get to be there for, a loyal dog, good friends and I'm spending my days happy and on my terms. That makes me a very rich man indeed.

I want you to think about what is really important you - I mean REALLY think about it. Then determine what your wealth is. I'm pretty sure you'll find it's not more stuff, but doing work you care about with people you love. Once you understand that time and not money is the greatest measure of wealth, you can adjust your life to reflect that.

Every single morning I walk my kids up to the front stairs of their school, kiss them on the head, tell them that I love them and send them off. They tell me they love me too, walk up the stairs, open the door, then pause to look back and smile at me just before they enter. It's at that moment that I realize, every single day, how very wealthy I am. Those smiles are worth more to me than any amount of money, and I get to see them every day because I've created a career and life that brings me those riches, every single day.

And so can you.

HAPPINESS

is the new rich.

INNER PEACE

is the new success.

HEALTH

is the new wealth.

KINDNESS

is the new cool.

22

Reinvent Yourself

I know what you're thinking.

"All this sounds great and I'm happy you were able to find a career you love and a happy life, Fern, but I can't do it because _____." (Insert your excuse here)

Here are some common ones I often get:

"I can't do it because I'm too old."

"I can't do it because I have a family to support."

"I can't do it because I'm broke."

"I can't do it because I'm too invested in my current career (education and time)"

Sorry, but none of those are stopping you. When I decided to follow my passion and make dogs my life, I was 38 years old (not a young man). I had no money, went to school for something completely different, my previous jobs had nothing to do with dogs, and within a couple of months of committing to learning to become a dog trainer, found out I had twin girls coming.

Despite all those things, I was able to create a successful career doing something I love and pin the needle on my happiness gauge. If I can do it, you can.

You see, unfortunately for me, my mom was wrong - I'm not special. I'm very much like you. I didn't have any special talents or exclusive resources. I wasn't sitting on a large nest egg of cash. I didn't know anyone who could help me accelerate my progress or make things easier for me. There was nothing really special about me or my situation at all, right?

Hold on a second . . .

Actually, now that I think about it, I am special. I do have some impressive skills. I can do amazing things.

The truth is, we are ALL special. The problem is that most people just don't realize it. Most don't understand that they have so much more than they are capable of and that they have everything they need right now to create an amazing life for themselves. The only difference between people living their dreams and those who are not as happy as they would like to be, is that the successful people woke up and stepped into their greatness, while the others just haven't realized what's waiting inside them. Look at me. I was a shy, unconfident, depressed, lost teenager and young adult. Who would have predicted that I would eventually write a self-help book?!?!

In addition to my love of dogs, I'm kind of a superhero geek. I was into comic books as a kid and now, as an adult, am first in line to see any superhero movie (I just watched Thor: Ragnarok last night - awesome movie, by the way). I think the thing that most appeals to me is the idea of the reluctant hero. Take someone like Superman for instance. Most of the day he walks around as mild-mannered Clark Kent, a normal person who looks just like everyone else. No one around him knows that under his business suit is bright spandex with a big "S" emblazoned on his chest. He hides what's inside, sometimes even from himself.

This may sound cheesy, but I really believe we all have an inner superhero waiting just below the surface. You - yes you - have so much untapped potential lying dormant inside you that is just waiting to be unleashed.

> "We are all capable of infinitely more than we believe. We are stronger and more resourceful than we know, and we can endure much more than we think we can."
>
> - David Blaine

There comes a time in every superhero movie where the reluctant hero finally understands what he can do and how it can be of use to him and the world. At that moment, the entire flow of the story changes. This is when the action starts, the music gets loud and all the story goes into high gear. It's when the movie gets good!

That's what happens to your life when you finally wake up and realize that you're capable of so much more. When you make the choice to leave your mild-mannered life behind and be the superhero you truly are (spandex optional).

The best part, and the one that most people don't realize, is that you don't have to be born with superpowers to be a superhero. Check out Batman. He has no supernatural powers at all. All of his amazing skills were learned because, as we know, "all skills are learnable". If you just figure out what you want in life, learn how to do it and go all in, you'll be a superhero in anything you want to do. Batman has his utility belt and gadgets, I have a leash and liver treats. We've both created careers and lives we love (P.S. Batman, if you're reading this, I wouldn't say no to an invite to the Justice League - just sayin').

I don't care who you are, what your current career is, where you live, how old you are or what your current financial situation is like - if you want a job you love and that makes you happy, it's available to you.

Just because you went to school for something or you've been working in a career for a number of years, doesn't mean you can't make a switch. If what you're currently doing is not making you happy, I would argue that you MUST make a switch. You can reinvent yourself - as many times as you like. I've had at least five different careers so far in my 48 years, and every time I switched careers, I went to something completely different and totally reinvented who I was professionally, not to mention my personal transformation from depressed introvert to outgoing speaker.

Something cool happens when you have a job you love. Once you're spending your days doing things that makes you happy and leave you feeling fulfilled, you do your best work. You enjoy it so much that it's easy to put in extra effort and you have more pride in the stuff you're producing, whether it's a product or service. And when you do your best work, people notice and things happen.

When I set out to become a dog trainer, I decided I was going to go all in and be the very best one I could be. I worked hard and people started to notice, bringing me more business and more opportunities. Following my passion and happily working hard at it opened up doors I didn't even know were there. I never thought that being an author, speaker, consultant (to dog businesses) and mentor (to aspiring dog trainers) would ever have been in my future, but because I followed what made me happy and did it well, all these amazing bonus opportunities arose.

Life is way too short to waste time doing something that is not enjoyable. The reason I had so many careers is that I would do something I thought would make me happy and then when it stopped making me happy, I moved to something else I believed would make me happy. This is where people get messed up. They do something for a period of time, realize one day that they really don't enjoy it, but the idea of leaving it (what is familiar) and trying something new (what is unknown) is scary. When you're comfortable with something and it's uncomfortable to leave, even though leaving would be for the better, you are experiencing the pain of disconnect. It's typically not the change, but the transition that we fear.

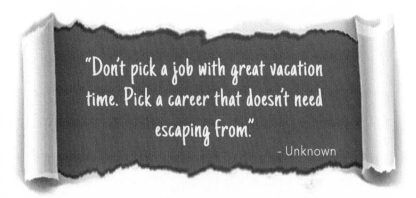

"Don't pick a job with great vacation time. Pick a career that doesn't need escaping from."

– Unknown

I'm not going to tell you it's easy to leave one career for another, it's not. It's hard work and will take some sacrifices along the way. I am going to tell you that, once you find work that you're passionate about and love doing, it's well worth the effort. Once you're on the other side, as I am now, you'll be so grateful you had the guts to make the change. If you're smart about it, you can lessen the risk by doing your homework, researching the career you want to switch to and finding the right mentors to help you get there.

Don't wait too long though, the clock is ticking. Remember, we only get one life and this is your only shot to make it as awesome as possible. Time seems limitless, but we all only get a very specific number of minutes on this planet and none of us know when our timer will reach zero, so we need to live every second like it was one of our last. Remember, "Every breath leaves me one less to my last." That's a line from a rock song by the band Dream Theater called, "Pull Me Under," that has stuck with me for many years, reminding me that our time here isn't limitless.

Don't put off your happiness. Don't delay living your dreams. Be happy now.

Remember, we learned that happiness is not about money (although that can be a part of it - just not the main part) and it's not about status. It's about fulfillment and purpose. What would get you excited to go to work every day and what would make you feel good after doing it? What would energize you instead of draining you at the end of the day? What would make you smile more and enjoy your work days?

That's what you need to do, and if I were you, I wouldn't put it off. Find your passion, bust open your shirt, reveal your cape and fly high. If dogs are your thing, reach out to me. I would be happy to help you turn that passion into a fulfilling, long-term career as a dog trainer. Whatever you choose, just keep moving toward the path that leads to your specific happiness, whatever that is for you.

Now up, up and away!

THE END

(but your new beginning!)

Big Take-Aways

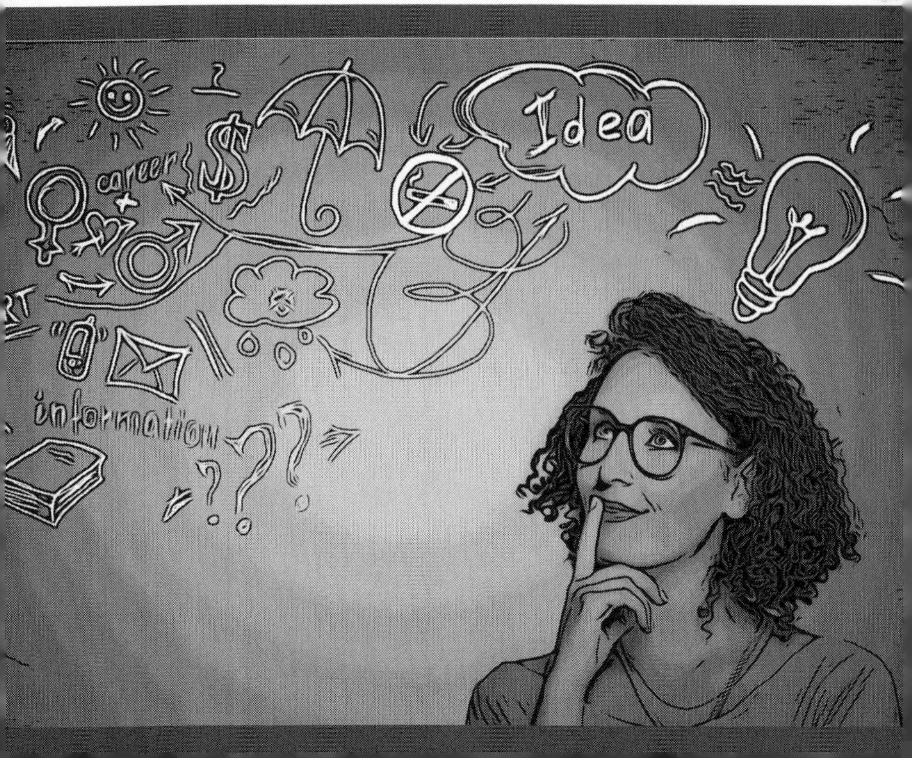
Idea
careers
$
information

- You can, and should, find work you enjoy.

- It's okay not to know exactly what you want to do "when you grow up." The way to find out is to identify what makes you happy and go in that direction.

- If you don't like what you're doing (or you did once, but not anymore) it's time to make a change.

- If you don't like where you are, you need to do something different. If you don't, nothing will change.

- When life kicks you down the stairs among the loose change, you have two choices: stay at the bottom and accept it or get up and start climbing, one step at a time.

- You are where you are in life because of your choices. Take responsibility for your past choices and make new choices that will better serve the direction you wish to go in.

- Negative things will happen to you that are out of your control; however, you are in 100% control of how you choose to respond to them.

- Obstacles are to be expected but not accepted. If you want to, you can choose to find a way around them.

- Always do the best job possible, no matter what the task. Work like what you're doing could greatly impact your entire life, because you never know when it might.

- Opportunity often looks a lot like hard work. If you want great things, you have to be willing to put in great effort.

- Your attitude will determine the lens you see your life through. If you're negative, your life will have a dark tint to it; if you adopt a positive attitude, everything will be brighter.

- Gratitude + Positivity + Excitement = Ratitude

- When you love your job, there is no Monday - only lots of back-to-back Fridays.

- Making money without fulfillment will not bring you happiness.

- Sometimes what seems like a stroke of misfortune can turn out to be the best thing to happen to you, once you gain a little perspective.

- Beware of jobs that make you comfortably unhappy; you don't hate them but you sure don't love them, either.

- Always remember, all skills are learnable.

- Finding the right a mentor will move you further, faster, and enable you to avoid all the common obstacles and pitfalls along the way to your goal.

- If you wait until you're completely ready, you'll never do anything.

- Planning, goal-setting, wishing and prayer will take you nowhere unless you take repeated action.

- Whatever career you choose, make it a practice. Keep your mind open, be receptive to learning new things and never think you know it all.

- Finding a part-time job within the topic of the new career you're starting will help you get a little money coming in and also provide you with skills and resources that will move you forward.

- Be clear on what your priorities in life are and make sure your schedule and choices reflect them.

- When looking toward a new career, relationship or anything in your life, don't look at what the average results are. Never shoot for average. Instead, look at what the top range of success looks like and do what's necessary to put you at the top.

- Don't be a flea and put a lid on your abilities. You are stronger than you know and can accomplish so much more.

- The only difference between a successful person and an unsuccessful person is that one gave up and the other kept going, even when times got tough.

- The more you put yourself out there, the more opportunities will present themselves.

- Work harder on yourself than you do on your job. Make personal development a priority to create the very best version of yourself.

- Be very aware of the language that you use and replace negative talk with positivity. It will create a ripple effect in your life.

- Always think colleagues instead of competition. Try to befriend your competitors so you can learn from and support each other.

- No matter who you are or what your situation is, you have permission to reinvent yourself as many times as you like.

- There is a superhero waiting inside you. Only you can suit up and step into your greatness.

- Redefine your definition of wealth. It's not having more stuff, it's doing things you enjoy, work that fulfills you and spending time with those most important to you.

- Your time is the most valuable thing on the planet. Treat it as such.

Acknowledgements

As I mentioned earlier, I start every day with a moment of gratitude, and the following people make that morning list quite often:

My parents for always supporting me in everything I've ever done. I know I gave them more than a few gray hairs as I figure out my way in this life. They are always there for me and I can't say "I love you" enough.

My amazing wife, Michele, who's always my biggest fan, but is also the one who reels me in when my imagination runs a bit too wild. She compliments me so well and is without a doubt my soulmate.

My delightful twin girls, Sabrina and Jada, who have shown me what real love is. I'm so proud to see the beautifully strong girls they are growing up to be (despite the many parental mistakes I've made over the years).

My super awesome editor, Rebecca Shipman, who is always there to fix my grammatical injustices and come to my literary rescue. I don't know what I would do without you.

Peter Gargiulo for not only his photographic skill at shooting the cover photo, but for designing the cover of this book as well. You rock!

Christine Gossinger for her proofreading expertise. It's so nice knowing I have you as my last line of defense to make my book the best it can be. Thank you so much!

All my friends, both off and online, who have added to making my own life a very happy one. Love you all.

And of course to YOU, who took the time to read this book - even all the way to the Acknowledgements page! I appreciate you more than you'll ever know and wish you a fun, exciting, rewarding, happy, imperfect life.

About Fern

Fern has discovered that his personal mission is to help people improve their lives - whether it's with their dog, their business and/or their life.

Locally, in New Jersey, he's a dog behavior consultant and trainer, where he spends his days helping people and dogs live together better. He also enjoys helping others turn their passion for dogs into a career in dog training, via his in-person apprenticeship and The FernDog Trainer Academy online program. Nationally, Fern does consulting with dog daycare, boarding and grooming businesses, using his varied experiences to enable dog entrepreneurs to improve what they do, have more success and serve more people (and dogs). Globally, Fern is a popular speaker at conferences and private organizations where he's always happy to share his message and connect with people all over the world.

Fern loves creating content, recording videos, podcasts and writing articles, blogs and books. In addition to this book, Fern is the author of *The Happy Puppy Handbook*, *The Dog Rescue Handbook* and one novel, *Dog Spelled Backward*.

All that stuff is great, but Fern's biggest achievement and focus is being a good husband to his wife, Michele, and a great dad to his twin girls, Sabrina and Jada (and let's not forget his Beagley buddy, Bowie).

For more info on Fern or to book him as a speaker at your next event, go to www.fernandojcamacho.com.

Join The Revolution

www.HappinessFreedomFighters.com

Made in the USA
Columbia, SC
28 December 2018